Faun

Faun © 2019 Brandi George

Published by Plays Inverse Press
Pittsburgh, PA
www.playsinverse.com

ISBN-13: 978-0-9997247-6-7

First Printing: October 2019
Cover art: "At the Riverbank" (1918) by Ivan Bilibin
Page & cover design by Tyler Crumrine
Printed in the U.S.A.

**PLAYS
INVERSE**

Faun

brandi george

Plays Inverse Press
Pittsburgh, PA
2019

For L.N., the Faun

NOTES

The book flinches like a school of fish, a murmuration, a murder nation, my colonizer's baby handprint on a paneled wall in a farmhouse in Ovid, Michigan. The book unearths burial mounds and flattens them into fields. My ancestors removed the bones, and I removed arrowheads from the creek, and I held them to my heart, and I searched the grass for blood, but all I saw was a starling. She hid her eggs in my chest, and when I drifted to sleep I saw black-winged, nameless shadows.

This is the Book of Lily. Lily Rail was my great-great-grandmother. I stole her photograph because she looked like my mother. Lily's eyes stared through me. Who was she? My history is as blank as the cornfields.

After I was raped, poetry became a golden labyrinth, and I stepped into the color world. I cleaved to each beautiful thing. As the starlings began to hatch, I had less room for myself. I was afraid of my visions. I was afraid of the colors and voices. And now I walk as Lily, wandering through a forest I'll never understand, speaking to creatures I have only seen in passing, through a landscape that has been obliterated and tamed and slaughtered and patched and re-patched.

Armed with a Celtic tarot deck, I began to identify more with the nonhuman than the human. I imagined trees spoke to me, shadows flexed their wings, and gnats carried secret messages from the underworld. The Book of Gnats. Earthworks swallowed me at night, and I became an enemy of the farm. I became an enemy of houses, furniture, mirrors, makeup, mattresses, matrons, patrons, patterns. I became an enemy of myself. I tried suicide, but I was an enemy to courage.

The book flinches like a starling, like the gun that shook in my hand.

PROLOGUE

Lily:

So it begins with a starling
   who lives in my heart as it lives in my mother's
as it lives   in her mother's   as it lives
 it grows round
                with night   as it lives
      it grows a blood red beak
& its eyes cast a shadow long groove
over us living & dying   the hatchlings'
claws scratch   scratch   scratching
the curve of skin on that pretty   pretty
    drum silhouette lush
field where blood gathers in pools   streaks
        sin & cinnamon   some new shades of lipstick

    I'm fourteen with long wet hair
the sun born in each wave   swimming
drifting   a few miles from my campsite
tired   like when I sat on my bed
   & slid the safety off a .45
pressed it   into my temple   surrounded
by wallpaper   cutouts
from magazines   Michelangelo
Raphael   the Ninja Turtle movie
          I saw with my father
I wasn't sure how to die
but I thought about it every
day

This time I beg Lake Superior
to swallow me   nothing happens   I turn
     to the shore   see a black bear watching
& I'm afraid to leave the water
         drowning is clean   the sea god
    waits in the darkness like a father

I dream over & over the bear's blue heart

      beating open chest   it slices

my face   kills the girl I was

Sometimes you go in one lake
and exit another   not a monster but a shed leaf
   sometimes you lose the light in your fingers
it's cold   not like a bombed city
not genocide starvation sickness   the sadness
is my mother's definition for fog
         clouds fallen from the sky

There are as many last breaths
as first breaths   in the forest with my eyes
closed   in the cornfield where I was   raped
in the trash pit where my father burnt my poems
      in the throat of my exorcist
      in the cold air above the baptismal water

Sometimes the world
   is created by sending one brave animal after another
in search of dirt

My cuts brush against my cut-offs
beneath my hair   a bruise   Hey West Wind
        beat your feathers against my arms

     Hey West Wind
         make me thy lyre

Wren liar   oak liar   pupa liar
sitting on my bed with angels
I hear my own name echo
shadow hair skinless face
superimposed over cherubs   hydrogen
liar helium liar carbon liar

stamen liar   cilia liar   xylem
liar   something split
                              what if
          my leaves are falling like its own?

At Hot Topic I buy pink
          hair dye   skip biology
                    walk to the cemetery
          with headphones swimming Nick
          Cave into gravestones spinning
                    we're already dead
          sad people with flats of impatiens

                    Now shipwrecks lift up and up

so even my uncle raises his healed skull

from the rocks   beneath the cliffs
of Lake Superior   his friends laughing
drinking beer   spelling insults with bottle caps

A red monster opens her mouth wilder & wilder
white   black   blue   horses

          disintegrate as the land

                    shrinks to a clump of dirt

clutched in a drowned muskrat's fist

ACT I:
LILY & THE BLUE-HEARTED BEAR

SCENE 1: OVID, MICHIGAN, 1994

Archer sees the buck, tabs his Western's page, and aims.

First Arrow:

>Antlers hook pine
>snake shifting shade
>prism o teeth cave
>
>spectral winter spine
>bark dead now mine
>red pine blade
>
>bolted eye maze
>blood leaf alive
>wake cell hive
>
>sun green rage
>muscle bow brace
>prism o teeth rise

Second Arrow:

>Haze hot
>archer
>waste shot
>whisper
>
>take not
>hotter
>skull pot
>spider

Buck:

Plasma amen
helios fire hymn

forests swim
crushed trillium

chrysalis, give me
aorta venom

lung dawn
dark stung home

Archer:

Sun in my hands I stalk
the sun in my hands I
stalk the sun in my
hands I stalk the sun
I am the sun Golden
Archer the One True

The Flower God, Crone Anemone, wakes.

Crone Anemone:

Buck, sink blood into earthworks, vine
red, twist into the shape
of a child. Stretch Lily's arms.
Split skin. Blue-Hearted Bear, restring ligaments,
sew fur on pulp. Limestone, harden
into hooves. Starlings, fold
your knife-black wings and beat
a syncopated rhythm.

Archer aims at the doe that was his daughter.

Doe Lily:

Red river
      pink leaf
sun sifts through branches
webs   needles
yesterday's rain
      squirrels' sweat   dust
stirred by cardinals' tails
     the wind carries
scent of human, old straw
        bow drawn
   the arrow grazes
   a ventricle's maze

       Holy Mother of Pines
       turn me to an evergreen!

Crone Anemone:

Fur, loosen. Skull, crack. Neurons,
snake. Frontal Lobe, fork into root-bundles.
Hair Cell, probe the dirt. Nuclei, spark.
Dendrites, stretch into xylem. Electricity, pulse
from underground. Drums, echo softly.
Brain-roots, grasp as leaves
sprout. Legs, harden
to bark. Hooves, elongate to tree limbs.
Blood, drip. Evergreen Lily, forget
that boy's hands and how he threw you down
among stalks, forget winged tennis shoes,
barrettes ploughed under in spring.

Evergreen Lily:

He said there was one door   I couldn't open
a test   so in the cornfield/castle-maze Chris said
"you can look" when he turned around to pee
      I did & ever after   fingers stained
with red blooms   tiny bitten hearts   cedar roots
blood warning   Ladies *O curiosity*
thou mortal bane   fairy key or egg stained
      red with the guts of curious women
& red with their severed throats   still questioning
why am I dead   why am I dead & the moon
doesn't give a fuck   silver dirtbag   no she
won't sweep the field   find our limbs   rearrange
our bones breathe   into us   so we are whole again

Crone Anemone:

Branches, shift. Limbs, crash and lift
to rain. Forget Chris. Forget the field,
the swell and burst of syllables:
Li-ly, loblolly, liriope,   layer aria pin,   lyre eye a pen,
live you are a pine!

Evergreen Lily:

To drift
        to luster
                to hum

hiss of pith
        hiss of vascular
                hiss of xylem

thought as auxin
        thought as leaf scar
                thought as bud

Crone Anemone:

Music, blue, rhythm unending,
dissonant. Wavelength, vibrate, color,
music, vision, wavelength, color, music,
color, wavelength, rhyme
in the rock-teeth, lizards in the rock-
mouth, fossils' vague death-stare
crashing on rocks' bloody incisors.

sky   sk   y
                                is
black   see   the   i   s   le
river   she   will   s ea   l
river   she   will   b e   e
 call   her   crushed   u n   c l e
  who   the   green   c   i rcle
              sore   open bled
     notes charged   crying into me
                             hands I am
      she's   eternal   now   violet clover
                             grayling passenger pigeon   O
      roots   where do we go after extinction
                             my new body my first body
       an   a   l e   p h
                             j   o   v e
     airy   e   v   e r
     flame   s   eam   her e
      in flooded   ti   me   s   he
 is shorelines   celestial graves   ye s   se e
bodies asteroids planets fire black until the dawn shakes the horns off her head viole (n) tly

A Robin perches on one of Evergreen Lily's branches, tells her a story about her grandmother.

Robin:

> Pam, whose bow pressed tight in her mastectomy scar,
> hunted Buck, his aura made of clouds.
> Pam loved to hunt. She knew the deer could read
> her thoughts, so she became the woods. Each dawn
> her being scattered through the leaves and leapt
> through sail-finned graylings, now extinct,
> in soybeans, hollows, brambles, caves, and dens.
> And so, at dawn, she tracked Buck
> through goldenrod, past Hawk's Pub,
> fishermen's boats, across Tahquamenon
> Falls, the river winking millions of eyes
> which she mistook for stones. Buck drank
> only from the coldest spring, where white
> erased the color from the earth,
> where cast-off antlers wore a shroud of snow.
> Pam got to full draw, then shot
> her arrow through his neck. He ran;
> she ran. He leapt; she leapt. He swam; she strapped
> her bow to her back and swam after.
> From shadow to shadow, she tracked him, until
> she couldn't tell her skin from his fur, her green
> from his black eye. Her oneness worked
> too well. As Buck died, she felt the wounds.
> And after, she lived as animals live.
> Now and now and now and now and now.
> When she drank, the pool gave back his face.

Crone Anemone:

Hand and hoof, fur and skin, mix
deer and human. Atom tangles, linger.
Matter, melt, and softly dress two wounds with water.
Kiss and arrow. Lovers, heal through transformation
when tongue is bandage. Birds, winter.
Winter, whiten ivy crowns, when the farmer's
heart is blankest, most beloved.

Archer and his wife, Optician, continue searching the woods for their missing daughter, Lily.

Fox:

> In the River's dream
> orange is a hollow
> of eyes hiding a summons,
> the last tree on earth
> lost in fire.

Kits:

> Long live Crone Anemone,
> origin of beauty!

Fox:

> In the River
> the vertebrae of a girl
> who never loved water
> sway while currents
> drum against carps'
> flaming scales.

Optician:

From flooded basements, rain seeping through mud,
from cases of Bud Light, a radio's broken waves,
from supreme pizzas, from silos where I leapt with stolen apples,
from wheat fields trimmed with blue cornflowers,
from pontoons' slow waves, the cacophony of ducks
rising bronze, light-drunk feathers!

Archer:

Shadow I am the bat god
of the meadow
as the woods near, I melt there
and my sleeves shade
into a leaf's blade

Optician:

Mysterious crickets in the twilight!
Mysterious purple of the darkness ringing!
What am I that the forest should part its lips,
unbutton greenly, reveal its sharp obsidian limbs?

Crone Anemone:

Rain, drip the lives
of forest creatures. Consciousness,
bleed music, billions of
(sharp). You, *(sharp sharp sharp)*,
but finally, *(in tune)*
infinite.

                    AA
          ink crossings or
        folk melodies
        l   e   a   v e
          l   i   f e
moral the human arc magnolias   fish rotted   orange
gold heavens chant   ever-falling   ancient empire
  the latch-oracle   cement night   falling   magnolias   rotted
                        sunlight squared   stones are
                        orange gold   falling
                        graylings surround   suckerfish
                          heavens chant   let her
                            delicate let her   evergreen
                        cone   let her   elongated

                                        waterfall

Fox:

Would you believe me
if I told you the earth's
spirit and form might be shattered
by a flower? That white
is a hollow of incisors, waiting
always for another mother?

Archer:

Teenagers are vacuums
drunk with no light a friend
will drop her the night will
swallow her merciless
teenagers are vacuums
drunk she'll exit the car
no apology no light

There is a bluish glow within the Foxes' den, as if they're watching TV. Archer smokes them out, discovering Crone Anemone's radiant root. When he touches it, callouses rain from his fingers.

Kits:

Long live Crone Anemone,
origin of beauty!

Crone Anemone:

Air, project membranes. Pines, shake. Forests,
hum with anemones. Time, stop, turn young, old,
zygote, corpse, then wait. Wait.
Now dirt and sing.

Root Song:

I heard it from Pure Green Vine:
Aeon when spirits change forms,
Unfolding with billions of eyes
into rivers and willows. It warned

this will summon the cell
whose waking created the worlds,
and sing of a time when elms
might transform into girls,

and girls melting to night,
and suns flying like moths,
and moths forgetting the light,
swell to agates, all lost,

not nameless, not named.
The genome pirouettes,
confused by the thing it became.
It's praying for serpentine breath
now nameless, now named.

Wolf:

Crone Anemone is easily stolen from Archer's wonder hands. At twilight, River heals herself with fish. Fish, too, shade in swallowed dragonflies. Gnat, Mosquito, and Damselfly crowd the water's surface. Fish wait and pucker, take insects back into wingless darkness. This morning we were afraid—the creature—River's song—biped stalking like thunder in the brush. And who awakened Crone Anemone from a hundred years of sleep, commands like thunder? And what are we if not gray, locked in fur, our eyes yellow as teeth? The rain fell from the man's fingers like Crone Anemone fell from the sky millions of years ago, ring of supernal light, circles within circles . . . But here is Gnat, always Gnat, alpha, omega, stirring from the swirls of our abandoned skins.

Gnat:

.

Back at the farmhouse, Optician rummages through a bin of her stillborn, Daniel's, old baby clothes.

Optician:

> Give me words to bless his body, to lift his quiet limbs,
> fragment his spine into sparrows' wings.
> Give me prayers that knit themselves into blankets,
> protecting and carrying him to a place where beasts
> green the sky, blue trees, feather oceans, stretch
> their muzzles to illuminate each other.
>
> Let Lily materialize heartbroken from a long walk
> through darkness, or drunk from a stranger's Chevy, or high
> with all the windows down and rap music booming
> and atheists hanging their tattooed arms out the windows!

River Lily: *(to the buzzing forest)*

> Every night Mother searches   for ghost brother
>   umbilical-choked   violet   sky-watcher
> while our alien ancestors search from on high
> for my blue magic cape   it's real magic
>   like clouds from endangered trees
>   like clouds released from the nostrils of March fawns
> like ultraviolet black daisies calling   lover
> to bees   the obvious invitation   sigh
>   of crickets between stringing & sparked steel
>   ringing from the garage   & up close fireflies
>   ugly crushable but fairy on the lawn
>
> where live you brother brother grown under gone?

Wandering home from the woods, Archer stares at his hands.

Archer:

> Shadow stalks where I can't
> against night against against
> working third shift at Sealed Power
> sun sparks from my hands
> all night steel rings
> around my neck
> wrists ankles   throat   fingers
> inside my head
> ringing inside rings
>
> when I think
> insides turn to steel
> lungs fill with oil
> shadow lives between
> ringing steel
> like church bells
>
> when I think
> I become Shadow
> thinking thinking foreshadows
> death so my God
>
> sleeps horses sleep
> women sleep
> forest sleeps
> while I forge myself
> from the sparks of a welder
>
> If I take off work
> If I take off my mask
> I'll burn my eyes

Owl:

Look, memory bumps, memory twerks
with angelic maggots as they loose us
from our forms. Archer, look!
They twist above the earth, Mnemosynes
of grass, and flow—not for what was,
what's dead—but wind, leaf, lake.

Mushrooms:

Crone Anemone:

Echoes, drift from night-mouths, float
as purple, ribbonous vapor. Archer,
stumble. Lily, sink
into the river, slither your green hair
behind you. Sea you downstream.

River Lily:

The forest remakes me   tears off my hands   rests
each digit on an ant maze   (for the will to survive)
then my eyes are two eggs in a robin's nest
    then my lips carved by hawks
then my sockets bluebird houses
then my skin a mask for raccoons
(so chaos always finds me)   while my feet are
aerated by worms my marrow
    absorbed by pines   (strong roots)
while blood sinks into ferns   ovaries
blown seeds   (now the wind lives in my skull)
dress washed downriver   so when it's spring
my cochlea may sprout

Robin:

The horned child, waiting for new life, hums
with eyes that spin a vortex that you'll never
shake, while news of transformations
wake the sleeping woods, mixing with the leaves
into the dark that isn't dark, but Debussy—

The color is the sound is C
sharp, racks carved into the trees.

The Blue-Hearted Bear drinks from River Lily.

Blue-Hearted Bear:

> Fear my claws
> Feel my paws

Satan   A demon
Smitten   A dream of

> Summons hell
> Sun on Hare

Hare:

Cracked from the egg of my stained-glass ribs

River Lily:

As the viceroy mimics the monarch's colors
    as the hawk-moth caterpillar mimics snakes
I re-applied my black lipstick after lunch
    & adjusted what one boy in biology
coined "the world's largest doily" which trailed
        on the linoleum as I wandered
the halls after the ache of the bell sang my starlings
       to flutter   lungs awake with each purple breath
I passed my hot economics teacher "You
            look like a clown" he said   & I exhaled

        The bear's heart burns blue
        The hare burns through

Blue-Hearted Bear:

> Cave of death
> Haven of dark

A sin   To repent
I sing   To reinvent

> All evil
> A weevil

River Lily:

I'm Pearl Prynne   Mother's "A" emblazoned
                        red fire on purple fire
    a changeling with weird luck   my elementary
school friend said "You are wicked I can tell"

            it's my fault   I guess   there is something
            dead in my heart   or my eyes   or my head

My parents thought I was evil too   my words
made of horns wrapped in letters   hey
Bear   hey   West Wind   what is darkness how do hive

       words twitch   crack their edges   pray

monsters into how   is my monster   how deep
its claws   my doubt   my questioning   evil birds
so they called her   Exorcist Cora   to kill   to lay
hands   good birds but

this isn't the story
                 forget it okay

Blue-Hearted Bear:

              Bad daughter
              Blue daughter

    Scarred girl   Possessed girl
    Sky girl   Purple girl

              Victim
              Vermillion

River Lily:

    Cora was Cora Goldman   will she sue
              at the edge of nightmares   Gold Goldman   gold gold
       archways leading to God

                        In a dream I took a bus to McDonaldland
          Cora opened a coffin   full of gems
    held a diamond in her fist   and pushed it through
    my eye & after I saw like
       a fly   with thousands of ommatidia
    mosaic   blurry
          she chucked me out a window   I can't fly
    falling until   fine kill me   then of course   flew
    over hills   houses   fields   Walmart
    all the clichés are right
          true greatness collapses   it's a fly in the night

Core of coral corral cornea color
        grass   I swallow   wasted
        fists of it   moss multitudes   algae
beds cloth   bags   t-shirts   sweaters
everything   grass   until seeds sprout puritan
blue & yellow flowers
        in my veins lungs brain spine nails hands eyes & hair
        in my antennae snout whiskers proboscis

I want to   no I'm crying   sudden terror
        when she sent her horrors out in clouds of fear

        Because Cora turns women into the undead, rank
            limbs contort pitiful hideous bruise-blue
corpse porn   another exorcist movie I
  flinch the familiar priest-hero's crucifix
brands her forehead her sinful decaying flesh
    lush rotting on bleached altar bones   owl neck
they hold her arms down   she's too strong   she's looming
    demon slut whore of Babylon   the hide
slips off her face   sinew muscle bleeding   sex-
        starved   wants to fuck her mother   how does the rush
of Christ heal her   torn hurt   desecrated breast

Blue-Hearted Bear:

Burn her
Braid hair

Snake night   With embers
Symphonic flight   With feathers

Riddles the girl with arrows
Rivers the girl with arias

River Lily:

Blue yellow red   primal witches riding what
  appears to be a man   long hair streaming   air-
fare free   dominating fornicating femme
  fatal & maleficium nightriders broomhags skinbags
familiars feeding from her hip nipple   poppets pinned
Satan-slut spoils beer & butter   but her betters better beware
       or she'll ride them like racehorses
speeding as fast as the earth or spacetime blur
          now she swings in midair &   now she's burning
         her throat a knot her arm a gritty wing

        now watch: her heart is blue with flame

Blue-Hearted Bear:

           A church
           A chirp

Madonna   Miraculous birth
Belladonna   Marigold breath

           The damned
           De-evolve

River Lily:

I used to steal everything   unicorns stove
      knobs miniature flags   polished rocks color

changing pens   cigarettes   & Pixy Stix   ten
     fairytale brothers   sisters & see   how I became
                               someone else
narrower   wider   a river flooding bold
 then drying up   the house decked with dream catchers
me on the floor   drunk   hallucinating phantoms
     now when I look into the mirror I can't

Recognize the shine   or the shadow   as mine
        I'm the wrappers my father chucks
out the window   of his pale Ford
        I'm the pale Ford
        I'm the horsepower
        I'm the rusted engine in the grass
                                in the field
                                the lane of abandoned machines

        I even stole my great-grandmother's photo
she hates me   but I love her she
        swells hotly in a starched dress   but did she cry
        body violet mind violet   & smoke
            like my mother to equivocate   recoil
            two snakes' sky-twined   sad refusal to give in
wasted mist of breath &   carcinogens   free
        as smoke or clouds   forget you   forget me

Some people can barely stay in this world   they lift like
        smoke or clouds   in the womb
I ate only eggs   then was born riddled with starlings
        & my soul is a feather   & my arms snakes' golden
    fuck you   bass shakes the house   fields my honor floods
        giant fuck you   is a zirconia sparkle
        & white trash middle finger   fuck is a swoon
                of starlings after
                                third shift at the factory cracks
        my father's ears   at sunrise   he stares down

        an infinite hallway   mornings stands in a cold
        deer blind & hums the soybean fields   as red as blood

                                The field cracks open. Lily jumps.

42

SCENE 2: NO TIME, THE INDUSTRIADS

Lily descends into the underworld.

Nymph Lily:

Death, to women, is a lover. To men he's an opponent. So nymphs are beauty-born, leapt forth from the first flower.

Chorus: *(each stanza at once)*

Robin:	Laurel and reed, harmonium
Robin:	Cedar in sleep, I'm home again
Robin:	Red wooden spine and veins of phloem
Robin:	Chlorophyll mind, the holly frond
Frogs:	Io—
Flies:	Daphne—
Fox:	Syrinx—
West Wind:	Eternally running—

Frogs:	Lolita—
Flies:	Echo—
Fox:	River aids the turning
Kits:	River reeds
West Wind:	The part you never see—after

Nymph Lily:

Nymph bodies stay hairless and sixteen. They are sometimes voluptuous, sometimes thin. They are: River Nymphs, Grove Nymphs, Forest Nymphs (dryads, and each tree has its own), Spring Nymphs, Sea Nymphs, Lake Nymphs (there is quite a difference between freshwater and saltwater nymphs), Mountain Nymphs, and Meadow Nymphs. Although some of these old kinds mutated into new breeds. Let's call them the Industriads: Radioactive Nymphs, Mine Nymphs, Skyscraper Nymphs, Junkyard Nymphs, Toxic Nymphs, Oil Nymphs, Assembly Line Nymphs, Cul-de-sac Nymphs, Trailer Park Nymphs, Inner-City Nymphs, Carbon Nymphs, Stump Nymphs, Dam Nymphs. These nymphs are mostly a result of the transformation of ancient habitats. These nymphs are restless from air pollution or remnants of prescription drugs in water supplies. They have too much estrogen, like the fish, and grow irritable. They lie beneath the earth, but sometimes their eyes (looking for all the world like a severed monarch's wing) peek from piles of broken bottles or the grill of a parked car.

Chorus: *(each stanza at once)*

Fox:	Floating in the lake
West Wind:	The hapless women of myth

Fox:	The hide's red-orange casing
Kits:	Hide red
West Wind:	Mouths becoming bark

Fox:	Barely keeps my body's
Kits:	Red my casing
West Wind:	Split their feet and search the dirt

Fox:	Water from the earth's
Kits:	Floating red-orange

Sycamore:

Sing then my Muse, now Eros Gaia sing,
Arrows sinking hot within skin languishing:
But Grammar's force now breath with breaks return,
For Grammar says (oh this deer's antlers sway)
For Grammar says (to Grammar sculpting clay)
That in one speech two Negatives affirm.

Nymph Lily:

Not no long-fingered phantom star and star lover. Not no vernal
equinox garland not no buzz. She maypole tears sheets. Did she not
bite? Did she not bloody scratch marks sweatshirt sober lock the door?
Did she not lava forest fossil? She's not nobody.

Sing then my not-unkind Muse, amuse my Muse, abuse me Muse,
you used old Muse, you cold prude Muse, you bruised Lover-
Muse, you fused Angel-Muse, confused Hegel-Muse, you pagan
Demon-Muse, you Martian-Muse, you silly Ruse-Muse, you groupie
Nympho-Muse. Hey Coke-Muse, get off it already, Joke-Muse.

Chorus: *(each stanza at once)*

Robin:	Sonorous ridge, the falling off
Flies:	Sappho
Robin:	Stone, and the killdeer's echo—
Robin:	I am creation, universe
Fox:	I turn into the first woman
Robin:	Scratching with scarlet fingertips
Frogs:	Some grief is too large and
Fox:	She, red-orange from copper
Kits:	She, orange-glow from the deep

Willow:

Woman, you are the gates of the body, and you are the gates of the soul.

Nymph Lily:

I hear the still-born animal hum, the vulture's carrion-cry, the catcall's prison of legs. I push against the boundaries of my skin. Is it my own? All of my mother's miscarriages, her abortion before I was born, her scarred uterus, the rape, STDs, the slick alien body. The limbs always remember, bones remember, ligaments remember. The rape-child before me remembers, the uterus remembers. I carry him in my muscles and joints, rape-child created in violence and torn with a hook. How I would be the only, all others slipping into mud. The gates of the soul are the gates of the body. The carnage of procreation lingers in the cell's division, the neuron's lightning, the soul already primed for war. Or if, when I was six, my close friend, like an older brother, threw me down in the cornfield, I would be one of many, disposable. A renewable resource of women springing from the body's gates.

Chorus: *(each stanza at once)*

Frogs:	Blood cells and bone marrow fail. Rivers
Bear: *(whisper)*	Blood water beats to the sound of
Fox:	He called
Kits:	He called

Frogs:	Change pain to mist. Brightly sun prisms
Flies:	Some grief is
Bear: *(whisper)*	Change pain to rivers. Some grief is

Robins:	Waves from the underground
Frogs:	Waves golden-red pearls on gray stones when
Deer:	Waves large from the deep, longing
Flies:	Too large and blood cells and bone marrow
Bear: *(whisper)*	Two rivers hide underground
Fox:	To give her the deep, longing
Kits:	To give her the night, longing

Willow:

> She's all states, and all princes, I,
> Nothing else is.

Nymph Lily:

> She's all states, all static, frenetic, C-R-A-Z-Y.
> He's autocratic, a speaker, persona. There's not no I in I, there's not no any in anyone. Run nymphs! There is not nothing more erotic, no? Io, white heifer caught between two paeans (that's the worst). And she's undone.

Chorus: *(each stanza at once)*

Robins:	Two wander North Star Polaris
Frogs:	Light wanders blue-throated saline
Deer:	Light rivers constellations
Flies:	Fail. Rivers change pain to mist
Bear: *(whisper)*	While rivers change pain to mist
Fox:	To see the constellations
Kits:	To see the far sun Polaris

Robins:	Rain prisms on little rocks
Frogs:	Rain softly green pooling breathe breathe worm
Deer:	First prisms gather on copper stones
Flies:	Sun prisms waves red
Bear: *(whisper)*	Sun softly waves pooling the stones
Fox:	Then she dries the copper stones
Kits:	Then she swallows little rocks

Nymph Lily:

Justice the Maiden tracks blood in. To keep it real, one must have
vodka. Who steps on gray shale burnt apples from battlefields? Who
touches cinnamon flint hollow ice cubes? Why Poseidon? Why Bill?
Why trident blue buzzing horseshoe? Why armor? Who searches for
you, Nymph? Who lights the neon camera flash heirloom? Whose
blunt? Whose mirror? Why bruises? Why torn heel dry throat poison?
Whose convertible? Whose diamond platinum cut-glass sun? Now
darkness, stairs, fast-beating wings, car alarms, basements. Where is
the emergency exit? Where is the love tiger Push Pop? You wished
yourself clouds, ether, wind, wildcards, wilderness, tinder, winter,
water, willows, lilies, licorice, limes, lemonade, luminous, lead. You
wished yourself dead.

Chorus:

Flies:	Change water change pupa-Jupiter
Bear: *(whisper)*	Change water change pupa-rivulet

Cedar:

The little Love-god lying once asleep,
Laid by his side his heart-inflaming brand,
Whilst many nymphs that vowed chaste life to keep
Came tripping by; but in her maiden hand
The fairest votary took up that fire
Which many legions of true hearts had warmed;
And so the General of hot desire
Was, sleeping, by a virgin hand disarmed.

Nymph Lily:

Metalmark. Hypnotize the sun
when nightmares' men, the shadow-hunters, chase—
Apollo's hot desire a speculum—
young women trapped with quicksand limbs. Erase
the shredded cloth, the satyr's horns adorned
with curls, the slow cruel lovely crush of palms.
Pink skin, pink heart, pink Heliconian ruins,
the red is gone, a woman's form embalmed.

Chorus: *(each stanza at once)*

Robins:	Sever the bridges and overgrow
Fox:	To make the summer sky
Kits:	To crack the summer sky
West Wind:	For power, in love with darkness
Bear:	For strength, in love with water

Robin:	Vines. Roads the roots shall fissure
Fox:	She smashes

Robin:	Asphalt, brick, and concrete. Oh
West Wind:	She hides until the Aeon of Subatomic Particles

Robin:	Wilderness, change forever my

Robin:	Petiole, antler, helium
Flies:	Lightning—
Bear: *(whisper)*	Lightning struck, burning pines
Fox:	Fire from the burning pines

Birch:

For every thing that lives is holy.

Every Thing:

For everything that lives is holy.
For everything that lives is holy.
For everything that lives is holy.
For everything that lives is holy.
For everything that lives is holy.
For everything that lives is holy.
For everything that lives is holy.
For everything that lives is holy.
For everything that lives is holy.
For everything that lives is holy.
For everything that lives is holy.

ACT II:
LILY & THE STAG

SCENE 1: OVID, MICHIGAN, 1894

Hemlocks:

Silver rush silver rush silver silver rush
Rush light aurora-crowned firebirds humming
The leaves are
Green flames in the eye
Lightning lightning chosen for the smoke-crown
Tallest straightest trunk in glory
Silvering bark hollowed to a V
This is how we
Honor apotheosize
Give glory
Lightning takes only the
Tallest wildest straightest
Trunk chanting change change
Fire change dust change ashes

Valence vacuum quiet
Change rush of darkness rush of pink
Night wings humming loud
Loud feathers thunder purple
Blue white gray schools of thunder-fish
Flocks flocking floating
Eating nesting graceful eggs
Eggs eggs in the dawn
Thousands of storm-bucks
Want racks of lightning scars
Of cumulonimbus then
Soft grass soft air soft hooves den of
Needles soft chlorophyll sleep

Have a red ever
Needles have a red
Head of need
Less spine-hollow backlit
Everneed
Birds dawn births threes
The eversinging red need of the sun sun sun sun
Sun sun sun sun billions of

Crone Anemone:

You, shred with questions:
Is there a god? Shred.
What is time? Shred.
Why violence? Shred.
Why did grandfather slip
a dollar in your pocket? Rags.
You would have died
if not for Christmas lights. Shred.
An old woman in the city
who never saw a star.
Rags of light.

Stone Lily:

Worship granite god, river god, pine god, maple god, butterfly, moth, punctured cloak of night, fish god, buck's crown of antlers, fawn, raccoon god, everything winged, chrysalis-born, egg-born, carrion birds, maggots, everything that dies in the light, everything that dies without light, shadow god, amoeba god, dark star, dark matter, fallen petal, needle tinted gold by the sun, the way light becomes a thing you can hold in the dawn, in the twilight, shelves of yellow finally spark on the almost-dirt needles. Earth earth earth, uncoil your coal snake DNA code timeless rift your snag in gifts of rage whole again I invoke you to open my ears lungs head open my skin open my skull crack open my rags of light my suffering open speak to me I am

Passenger Pigeons:

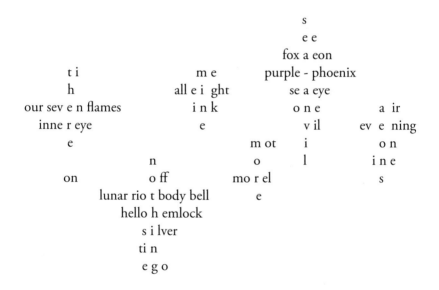

Sugar Maple:

A world, benign, cracks
Blinks slick wood silver earl
Curls the violet's tamarack
Ducks license luster hurl
Ears slow wave-*psh* of sand
Fronds break the shingled curve
Gives slick green-velvet land
Hands carved with star of nerve
Inverts the short-lived arrow crag
Jag of beach, storm above

Kelp tsar, kettle tsar combs
Looms of spacetime's cilium,
Meanwhile harmonic booms
Numb air. And the hive-ilium's
Orion-cannons thunder
Passenger pigeons! Their dreaming
Quill-crowned edges pour
Roar sonic bass and scream
Seams of slate-blue coral
Tempests, feathers stream
Umbilical ejecta, crag
Veined plumes in free-fall
Waterfall pinion
Xylem's burden crawls
Yellow amber sap, eggs, and
Zigzag of beaks among the twigs

White Cedar:

One's leaves must be composed of sulphurs.
Defy gravity with a wound, bloody roots.

A fawn leaps. Children crouch in the underbrush
dressed in its mother's skin.

Constellations become visible to beings
with eyes, the rest of us feel them
as waves.

One, two. One, two. Velvet soft,
the fawn's lashes.

A girl presses her nose to the bark
of a three-hundred-year-old white cedar. Me?

The procession of seasons, ritual of mitosis, mushroom ring.

Flex, flex, flex. Not every moth flies into the fire.

White sulphurs mobilize the flooded forest, the fluttering a mercy for the
swollen trunks. Ants Lily carts the twitching appendages on her beady backs.

Ants Lily:

> Because we eat beauty, we welcome destruction.
> White men gift the Ottawa a wooden box
> inside a box inside a smaller wooden
>
> box. It silences the horn-cut fawn.
> From each raindrop sings a pocket watch.
> Because we eat beauty, we welcome destruction.
>
> When the elders open it, their origin
> collapses into the cedars: smallpox
> inside a box inside a smaller wooden
>
> coffin in a grove inside the burning green.
> Ten thousand die, while lumberjacks
> eat beauty, welcome destruction,
>
> and soon the tribes, the pines, and pigeons
> will disappear, remembered by the rocks.
> Inside a box inside a smaller wooden
>
> dollhouse, white settlers' children frown
> into the painted likeness of a miniature hawk.
> Because they eat beauty, they welcome destruction
> swelling in a box inside a shrinking wood.

Crone Anemone:

You, eat the rival
queen's swollen body.

White Cedars:

Sincerity is like fire. Love remains the decisive failure, which means
food; food means survival, survival means family.

Suns also explode. The untested laugh. Snakes earn roundness in their
heads, while shells are picked over and sold, trapped in mason jars and
attics.

_____, _____, _____, _____, _____, _____, _____.

Desire uniformity of limb. Yearn for fragmentariness
and wholeness.

My sapling catches sun.

Queen Lily:

There are hands all over my skin. They suffocate me.
They want to teach me something, to impress me.
They want me to call out for a hero; they want me to yield, finally,
the human. They are tearing me to pieces;
they are putting me back together like a very difficult puzzle,
a very easy child's puzzle.

There are men in the shadows, in the light, saying,
I will kill you if you go into the light. They tell me
You asked for. You wanted. You didn't have to look.

They ask *Are you brave? Courageous? A woman? A girl?*
They want to tear my skin they want to nail me   kill me
kill it   and the forest burns the forest burns.

Millions of acres burning.

Fire Lily:

Auricular oracle, the altar altered awfully
       aweful, the loon's lunar offal. Cymbal of birds,
lune symbols whirring, worlds our whirred word, hours
     gnawed, the airy nod of a god's aerial heir errs,
bolder, boulders seized by seas of flame, hymns
       hummed by him who sees the bees in fame. Oh be,
profit prophet owing morals to morels, who blames
    the racked days of wracked lichen on dazed lumber barons
wearing eyelets, their jacks' lumbars cracked
       from stacking boards on barren islets. There, they're
bored until they feel the untilled fields ablaze. Liken them
    to blades of flame, waves waving over vales. Pray
for sheer veils of rain to shear the fire that preys,
      praise the lightning's muscle lightening, the mussel
graying, the dear deer that grazed.

Smoke:

Change trillium, change black squirrel, change pheasant,
leaves nearing autumnal glory, red and orange
change, flame-colors fade.

Fire Lily:

To war. Win. Winning. Won. One. Whir.
      Were you whole watching woe soar where the yew's
root-hole smokes, sore swords spore-smote? Whoa-ridden
      ewes' spoor ash, riddles of worn wool riddled with fairy
sparks ferrying through the dawn, the pale sky a pail
      of thrown ashes, ashes, ashes, our hour of animal mews
amusing morning's coral seam, what seems
      like choral mourning. Wrest the ring of need that knots
the hart's epic heart, the hare's hairy epoch laid to rest,
      not wringing for naught, no laze of kneading rays, just sun
leis raised and razed sons. Know the nose of justice chased
      the chaste night knighted by titans' soulless stares.
It tightens what the solitary cloud-stair's solace bears,
      the bared waste of tents, the tense bear's slow roll,
the waist of noon's gilded gills of gold, a pause
      of paws, the human role, the bow, the bow, the bough.

Ash:

Bouquets flare into darkness,
snake-rain, poison-coil,
twig-fire. Stop. Give me a single net.

> *Where do languages go*
> *after extinction?*

The space of. Before a mirror-
spoon, hawks pass, formless
oaths sworn into the smooth stone

> *Where do cultures go*
> *after extinction?*

of winter, fleshless, beyond
numb. Termites hunger, tangible
nightmares, love-note howls.

> *Where do species go*
> *after extinction?*

They want an arc, a luster-cosmos
of artifacts, a waxwing glassed in
and humming with underlife.

> *Into mountains.*

Lightness drifts, someone mentioned
hickory, locust, tin roof, meager.
You shall feather-trance as cursed

> *Into marshes.*

planets scar the hour, glittering
dense as banked coals. Smoke chalks
corpse-zero, letters vanishing,

> *Into bedrock.*

villages departing, puffs of breath
featureless, iron ligatures
the color of disciples.

Earth's Molten Core:

```
                am     en
             o grand   mother
         I regretful o  val halla
         battleaxe crow  n of helmets
        none is              luckier
        thorn               white
        wash    <1    1>    ed en
        long     2          blue
        black    2          hair
         in      44         the
        sun                 sun
        sun      88         sun
        but                 here
        the                 sun
        the  1        7    6 photo
        end                 beg
                            in


        s                   s
        p                   t
        l                   a
        i                   r
         t
```

Ash:

The farmer's pen whitens motion.
Embroidered, inextinguishable, eighteen
strangers walk in dead shoes.

> *Where does love go*
> *after extinction?*

Yesterday you invented a pillow-perfect
oval, nailed a portrait of temporality-
crystal. Gnash-drift, burnt-cave,

> *Will the earth*
> *speak to us again?*

applause, map of a temperate
bed, stillness cure and sign infertile.
Oh witness, shudder, Lethe-wind

> *Did the earth ever*
> *speak to us?*

enemies. Say hello, heavy habits
somehow panting. A spine of horizon
on this road I long for

> *Into eggs.*

lake-grace, sleep of ashes,
an Audubon mask transfigured
into sheet-metal nerves. The book of.

> *Into blood.*

Survive the coming horizon,
flightless rectangle, talon of absence,
demon-boiled wilderness. Stop

> *Into sandcastles.*

my love-paper-lungs, my emerald shovel,
my region of bullets, my aperture, caul
tender-eaten, my asps flourishing and doomed.

But the fire does not spread to the stumpfields.

White Pine Stumps:

> White pines have red gold pink auras 500' tall.

> White pine stumps have OCD (Orphic Crenelated Delirium).
> They do everything in fives.

> White pine stumps desire a glorious death by wind or lightning.

> O, sweet everlasting Voices, be stumpfields.

> Stomataphobia, xylemphobia, whorlphobia, rootphobia, axephobia,
> spidergarden, hollowgarden, splintergarden, sawgarden.

> Stumpfields never hurry. Atom by atom, little by little they
> achieve their work.

> In summer, the stumpfield sings itself.

> Our profession is to always find God in stumpfields.

White pine stumps, densely root-hooked, last for hundreds of years.

White pine stumps have no mother. They are paranoid lyrophobes.

White pine stumps are the inverse of decapitated heads.

The greatest wonder is that we can see these stumps and not
wonder more.

White pine stumps form an alliance with the grass.

They went to the stumpfield because they wished to live deliberately.

White pine stumps age into jagged holes; if your eyes travel into them
they are lost for years.

Thou shalt not white pine stump.

Stumpfields are the shadow of the farmer the shadow of the farmer.

In the depth of winter they finally learned that there was in us
an invincible stumpfield.

At the center of the imagination's dreamfield is a stumpfield.

White pine, pinus strobus, pine us strobe us.

A wilderness of stumps is impossible to imagine.

They come more and more to the conclusion that stumpfields,
in America or anywhere else, are the only thing left.

But there are always stumps for those who want to see them.

Lumber, paper, furniture, screen, hedge, doors,
paneling, boxes, crates, ship masts, shade,
oxygen, coffins, oxygen, matches, cabinets, boats, fence,
landscape, reforestation, antiseptic, Christmas tree,
reforestation, firewood.

The stumps are lovely, dark and deep. But they have promises
to keep, and miles to go before they sleep.

White pine has a pyramidal or oval crown. White pine
has a fast growth rate and height of up to 120'. The leaf type
is simple. The leaf shape is needle-like (filiform). The leaf venation is
parallel. The soft blue-green needles are borne in groups of five.

But it can also happen, if will and grace are joined, that as they
contemplate the stumpfield they are drawn into a relation, and the
stumpfield ceases to be an It. The power of exclusiveness has seized us.

Crone Anemone:

You, fly through forests & settle
on the roof of a lumberjack's shanty.

Fever. Ditch. Moan.
When Jack fells a pine, the sap
becomes his blood.

Jack:

A man cuts, drives the axe
parallel to the earth
with his back
in an arc like a trout,
the kind of moon
where a boy might hang
his visions. A man
braces, spits, gazes, squints,
pockets his hand. He
knows as the wind knows,
listens through his feet.

Jack: *(with guitar)*

Oh Lily the lightning and river-song girl,
Would stand on the banks of Tahquamenon Falls,
Watching her hands stretch as wide as the paws
of a blue-hearted spirit bear.

Hurray the dawn, the flaming sun.
The river's run with trunks of pine.

And Lil' used to run through the white pines and leap
off branches into the Grand River's deep.
She never wore dresses or shoes on her feet,
Until the pines disappeared.

Hurray the dawn, the flaming sun.
The river's run with trunks of pine.

So Lil' heard a lumberjack singing an aria
He said that he traveled from Upper Bavaria.
His eyes were as blue as the three-stringed aorta
of the blue-hearted bear from her dreams.

Hurray the dawn, the flaming sun.
The river's run with trunks of pine.

Crone Anemone:

You, skirt the shanty's edges.
You, re-evolve,
ascend to feather and fur, leap
into salmon. You, search
for me, Sacred Flower of the Eleven.
Swim through underwater tunnels. You, you, you
wait.

Fox:

A vowel mars each petal—
bridges for Man
to enter palest pink,
fingers outstretched,
trusting a reflection,
the chaos of
a blueberry rolled:

                    A

        U   Y   E

            O   I

I have loved
to drink from water-filled tracks,
and puddles where confused toads,
thinking the water permanent,
left tadpoles.

I have known the shadows
of cricket figures as
fireflies' electric odes,
as light feathered in warm patches
beneath the maple's canopy.

A snowy rock beats
its mammoth heart as if
we haven't done this all before.
As if all matter doesn't begin
with touch.

My hairs stand as gods,
white-throated and armed with ticks.
The night eats
what is unable to take wing:

        Arctic
        grayling

Upland   Y   Eastern
boneset   Elk

    Ornamented   Incurvate
    pea clam   emerald

Crone Anemone:

The Eleven—Bird, Sky, Insect, Reptile, Rock,
Fish, Mammal, Fire, Water, Rodent, Flora—
meet at the river, circle eleven times.
Reflect my light. Form a vision
of Oracle-Moose, made ancient by the leaves
of birch and pine, maple and hemlock. Shine,
leaf-seams.

Oracle Moose:

To cut, to shine, eleven times
eleven years beneath the dirt
I've heard the lovers' cliché rhymes
and mankind's oratory burst
the shell of logic with their crimes
against the pigments of the earth,
which scorch their eyes in wingéd code
the seven-tinted levels of the soul:

Red-buzzing-spindle-bud,
Orange-lightning-clover-scale,
Yellow-moon-blowfish-mud,
Green-crater-raindrop-prayer,
Blue-turtle-stamen-flood,
Violet-paw print-sulphur-hail,
Black-birdsong-limestone-sea—
the smallest pea's brain-symphony.

They'll break the forest's velvet sleep
with axes, fires' glowing eyes.
With fingers feathered omens deep,
while breathing, river, river, why
and how and what their digits creep
with numbers, dead machines that fly,
then river, river glowing blush
of sadness, killing darkness lush.

They'll trap us: petrochemicals,
acrylic, polyurethane,
dense, tensile, imperishable,
finely-tuned polymer chains.
We'll hug the ground as sauce-stained bowls
impervious to rain or sun.
Our bones will blacken in the cracks
of garbage bins and paper bags.

Grayling ghosts, forgotten fugue,
lumberjack, log, and hook. Buck
whose antlers number twenty-two
will crash the two-legs' temporal luck
and fold all creatures' blackest blue—
grayling ghosts, the galax-crux
trans-minnow mud, the acorn
sprouting fish-dust form.

Crone Anemone:

Aeon of Trees, change
to Aeon of Subatomic Particles.
Eleven, elect
Fox, most hunted & therefore
most prophetic, to guard me
until 1994, when we return.
You, justice is slow & amoebic,
eternal. Robin,
eat worms. Moth, wriggle
from your chrysalis. Wild Rice
Seedling, burst.

Lumbermen, sing. Timber, sing
timber sing sing sing.
No ears. Lumbermen
sing with axes. So
Hemlocks crash, the three
conjoined trunks split
the Sisters-Tree, the lyre tree. Crone
Anemone, shrink to a root. Foxes, gather.
Council, scatter. Roots,
send visions, dream
into the mask of my name.

Root Song:

I heard it from Red Wolf Cave:
The aeon when infants grow horns,
when calling the dead river's wave
wrecks parallel rows of corn.

In Ovid, the buck will run
away from Archer's bow.
His daughter hums Debussy's "faune"
while Faun becomes her zygote.

In Ovid, their daughter turned
into a pine, a doe,
a river, quick to learn
a moment's liquid flow.

Go back through waves of summer,
then forward through the ice
to save us from disaster
you need to jump back twice,

then summon the Blue-Hearted Bear.

Crone Anemone:

A   A
l tooth   burial l
l   protects   mound   l
  a   cave fang   incisor of   a

fossil prophet

sleep white winter fish bone mouth buried love hibernate
eight eyes beneath dirt curtains where is she

where   wear
b   b

my great sleepless ruin girl my claw of light

blue- black
chrys alis
o o

there is no death
like the one
I braid

SCENE 2: NO TIME, EIGHT EYES

Crone Anemone:

Fox, hide deep within
earthworks, summon
Eight Eyes, the newly-dead pines'
long-dead beloved. Call her: Claw Who Grips
the Earth, Skull Animal Hands, One
Ear. Call her: Thousand
Shadows, Fall Spring, Lightning-
Hollowed Pine, Crowned
With Fire, Air Phantom,
Raindrop Syllable, Nine-Minded
Night, Crotch of Fawns, Sugar
Beetle, Trout Marsh. Eight Eyes, wake!
Blink Lily's skull sockets, monarch wings, shoulders,
forehead, and navel. Blink golden
as a puddle. Fire, rise
from Lily's abdomen. Shadows,
loom from her birch-bark arms.

Eight Eyes:

Sunspot dries Limb Crusher's translucent
parallax. A thread for every year I wait:
one thousand. The bay will turn to a waning moon,
and then I'll climb the towering dunes
alone. Why does the tendril
wilt in subsoil? Gone, my tall brother
and my sister's clumsy footsteps,
the river where I gathered visions.
Sometimes I think I'm ants in pine bark.
Sometimes I think I've forgotten the luminescent
trail through white cedars where constellations rise.
Gone, the half-moon bay, banded agates,
the great copper boulder glinting sea foam!
White Pine! Maple! Hemlock! In summer women
swell inside the earth and roots anchor their hips.
In winter sea snakes sleep in clouds of slush
and lick their icy cages. A thousand years of red-
stained hillsides. Five lucid dreams
and a million million shovels. The circle breaks.
Gone, the brave. Gone, the Deneb Vega heart.

Crone Anemone:

You, follow Eight Eyes' voice
into shed feathers,
shrink & lengthen into Blue
Racer Lily. You, slither.

Blue Racer Lily:

Sacred objects dwell in mystery   must live
in blue   like when my poetry journal
            was given to pastors who pronounced them
Satan-authored   they were stored in a blue box
            until they were burnt still alive inside the plastic
            blue box   which cost twenty dollars &
before that relatives asked to see them   trembling
    at the thought of cursed/devil pages
a rare danger & my exorcist
                                        (Cora) said
there was once a girl whose black magic book
        manifested again and again unburnt by fire
she said the witch's indestructible book always returns to her

            it will survive   pure   intact

            if she believes it can't be lost

Eight Eyes:

Claw, lamb, tooth, vein, sound is fire and metal.
Claw, lamb, tooth, vein, the lake is a lava throat-bowl
clinging to ordinary light, a swan's neck clinging, held under
by a claw. Lamb, tooth, and vein, I'll eat her in the morning
when sound unspools the fiery swans, and lava lights
the dirt inside my veins.

Crone Anemone:

You, stretch-soften-stretch into a winged serpent. Swallow
enemies & sweep spirits past the atmosphere.
Grow into eleven celestial orbs:

Head, breasts, shoulders, hands, womb, thighs, and feet.
Become an eye of violet calling First Prophet,
Sky's Love Letter to the Trees, Flute Tongue,
Rail Girl—

antimatter	matter
chaos	order
gold snake	silver snake

micro	macro
buzz	point
=	lake

From stellar nebula into sun, red
giant, planetary nebula, white dwarf, black dwarf, blue racer, stellar
nebula, sun, red supergiant, nova, black hole, tadpole.

SCENE 3: OVID, MICHIGAN, 1794

Robin:

Now Lily floats back down to earth, her scales
receding as she once again grows limbs.
Her fingers pink, her hair begins to sprout.
A human girl, now Lily feels the cold
club moss splay between her toes.
Her Celtic tarot deck grows roots and lifts
the Stag, her favorite card, into the forest.
Displaced in Michigan, he waits in silence.

Lily:

Hello?

Robin:

The darkening forest answers with a single
cricket. Lily wanders all alone
through pines so tall they make her dizzy. Trees
resound with frogs and sparrows, louder, louder.
She sprawls beneath a tree and cries about
her former life, her mom and dad and friends,
the theater practice missed—who will be
cast as Juliet? Who will she kiss?
Will she die here? Is this death? Her dream
outlasts the night. The moon itself grows oval
like an eye and blinks. She hears a rustling
in the bushes, sees two glowing eyes,
and scrambles to her feet. She runs through brambles,
tripping over roots, splashes through a shallow creek
and slips. Her head crashes on the bank,
but still she crawls until her consciousness goes blank.

When Lily wakes, she's in a den of branches,
At first, she tries to rise but can't. Her head
rings, and her ankle is wrapped in herbs. She's scared
to stay, but more afraid to leave. The dawn
rings the earth with coral. She sees a man's feet
and ankles at the entrance of the den.

The Stag:

Calm. Won't hurt.

Robin:

But the strange man's legs are thick
with muscles, his feet too hairy. He wears a kilt.
She slinks away, brandishing a stick.
The man stoops low, and she sees his silhouette:
A stag! She screams and kicks, and as the dude
ducks low she tips the boiling pot and burns
her foot. Now the creature grabs her arms
and holds her still. He's larger than any man
she's ever seen. His body is like a human
male until the chest, which halfway up
grows fur. His neck and face are animal—
a stag's eyes and mouth and ears. He licks
his nose to keep it wet, and Lily faints.
She's fearless when she changes into
other beings, but when she is herself:
she cowers. While Lily sleeps, he heals her feet.

Stagman:

Hi.

Robin:

The Stagman growls when Lily wakes.
She swats his face with her open palm, and he
moves branches from the entrance of the den.

Stagman:

Fine. Leave.

Robin:

Reverse psychology.

Lily:

What are you? Where am I? What's today?

Robin:

Stagman puts his finger to his lips and shuts
his glowing eyes, and Lily hears a singing,
the sound of crickets keeping time and deep
within there is a wasp-like hum.

Stagman:

No ears?

Robin:

He picks her up. Outside the polestar shines
its light and fireflies flicker when the water
creatures change their key. She sees the mound
where Eight Eyes lies. She sees the river
and the hill where her farmhouse stood—will stand?
The pine trunks are larger than her arm span,
the maples too. What kind of thing is she
to see, miraculous, this healed earth?
This wanderlust, amphibious and joyful,
the grass's bendy open darkening lungs?
The Stagman concentrates, his eyebrows knit.
He's thoughtful, handsome … she thinks, *No way …*

Lily:

Who are you?

Robin:

The starlight shifts, illuminates
his antlers—forty-four. The starlight grows
to form an arc around them, glinting from
his antlers like a crown. She's in awe.
The woods grow silent, waiting. He clears his throat.

Stagman:

Guardian.

Robin:

He brushes constellations from his brow.

Stagman:

What?

Robin:

He shifts uncomfortably as she stares,
licking his nose to keep it wet.

Lily:

Dunno.

Robin:

Lily thinks, *stay cool, stay cool,* but damn
this guy is weirdly beautiful. The starlight
bends to form a bridge from Stagman's head
to hers. The bridge is made of colors, the colors
made of notes, the notes are made of letters
and the letters sing in colors brighter than
the human eye can hold. She sees them through
the stag. She sees them with her ears. She hears
them with her throat. She feels them with her tongue.
The Stagman's eyes are closed, and Lily reaches
out her hand to brush his hairy chest.
The Stagman jolts.

Stagman:

Return.

Robin:

He walks away, but Lily chases.

Lily:

Wait!

Robin:

At the river, Stagman stops to drink,
while Lily can't believe the reds of sunrise
on the water. She thinks the ribbons are
her heart, its beat, its double bar, repeat.
A burning creature is alive in her.
It rears. It scoffs. It laughs in gorgeous wicked
scales. It is a river's laugh within.
It's blue-black cosmic fire. Each breath entices
oxygen to fuel the flame. Each inhale
is an azure-dripping globe, finite
and fragile. Now breath is celebration and
grief. Now breath is paradox. The Stagman
pauses to regard her standing pierced
by water's morning palette. Here beauty
burns. Here beauty kills her consciousness.
Here beauty drags her ego through the mud.
Beauty born, beauty cut, beauty bruised,
her tears are wounds, the sky shredded (soon)
by airplanes, the forest cut, the farmer's fields
like scars. She checks her wrists—uncut. She checks
her eyes—intact. Her heart still beats, so how
has she been killed and who remains? Stagman
takes her hand and pulls her through the current.
She wears the river like a dress. It belts
her waist. She wears the river like a crown.
It rushes in her nose and mouth, while Stagman
holds her close. She rests her head on fur
and knows her flesh is in her head. She turns
to algae, river stones, and rainbow trout.
The Stagman, like a statue, stands. Now Lily
settles back into a girl, but fluid,
changeable enough to heal. She steps
back from Stagman and pushes up.
The breath she takes is like her first,
spitting water from her mouth, she coughs
while swimming to the bank and awkwardly
climbs up. The Stagman smokes as if he never
moved. But when he turns his head there are
eleven stars inside his bark-brown eye.

Stagman:

This isn't Scotland. Where am I?

Robin:

Lily points to a cloud with Stagman's
face. The white mouth opens to a howl—
out springs a wolf. She jumps and feels her throat.
It's raw, and her voice becomes a growl.
She's everywhere—her eyes beneath a rock,
colored like a shoreline. Her fingers, inchworms.
Her body shakes and suddenly, she coughs
out nine wet cocoons. Stagman helps
her line them up to dry, and soon, luna
moths emerge in leaf-green wonder. Then
she feels a flutter in her womb, and from
below nine chickadees emerge.
She cleans each bloody-feathered bird
on the band and holds them to her ear—

Chickadees:

Awake! Awake!

Robin:

Now Lily's fingers flex. They fly away.
Now gaining courage, Lily trails her hand
over the Stagman's arm. He turns his head,
but Lily gently guides his nose toward hers
and kisses wayward hairs between his eyes.
The Stagman's fingers flex—he doesn't move.
Now Lily smears the blood between her legs
onto his chest and grabs his antlers.

Lily:

By holy death, red sunflower.
By holy breath, black Robin.
By wings speckled, speckled April fur,
By scales speckled, mother's speckled eye.
By all the winds, and rain, and thunder breaks
I call you mine. I call you mine. I call
you many-headed hydra, sea beast, crown of daisies.

Robin:

With that she rolls her hips, and flips
her matted hair and Stagman feels her power,
life-lightning, birth-flood, and blood-
petal, rising. He pulls her on his lap,
and she wraps her legs around his waist and arches
her back until her hair touches the sparkling
gravel, ice-cut mountains, and the Stagman
holds her spine. The sky grows thick with rain,
which gathers on their skin in pools where fingers
grip. When the white bolt touches water,
they feel it as a name, a single syllable,
a moan in the back of the throat, a drumbeat.

Robin:

When Lily wakes, the tarot card blows past,
now shining through the opening of a cave.
She moves into shadows, wondering
where the Stagman went. Now she stumbles
to her feet, unsteady. The river rushes
past. On a far hill she sees the profile
of a buck. Hoof prints lead away
from the cave—no human feet. When she
looks again the buck is gone. And now
she shouts again. Her words just echo
back. She notices her foot is healed,
her energy is spun in fiery webs,
Her spine's serpentine scarlet threads
hum, ready to unravel sacred
helices to the cool morning air,
which lives inside another purple dawn.

Lily ventures out to find some food.
At the river, Bee Lily finds herself
within a bustling hive, while warriors
gather pollen from the buttercups.
Lily feels herself as many buzzing
far across the land. At night, she settles
in a hollow log—two hundred thousand
strong. But in the morning, something cracks
her home, nosing honey capped in cells.
A bear growls, consumes her work, immune
to stings. Behind a fern, a red fox beckons.

Fox:

Transform yourself.

Lily:

But how?

Fox:

Invite the West Wind into your lungs.

Robin:

Although she's human, although she's she, her spirit
vaults into the bedrock. A string, it sinks
from her, while she lets the tears run down
her face. She cries because the sky is blue
and infinite, for the miracle of falling
water, for clouds' dynamic faces, for time's
brutality, the love she feels already
for her multiplying child. But Lily's
soul snaps upward like a pea and shakes
with the noise of bursting suns and whirring
planets. To be strong is to be fixed,
immobile, set, unchanging. To be strong
is artifice. The rocks are changed by wind.
She's not interested in strength. Her tears
are made from oceans. Her heart, tectonic plates.
Her tears turn her to vapor, so she drifts
into the trees and grasses, birds and insects,
ready for another incarnation,
unafraid of death, unwilling to hurt
another being. Life is sacred. It
sings to the eye as beauty, sings to the chest
as joy, sings to the ears as an orange dawn
of crickets, singing, "Listen! Listen! Listen!"
But this is all cliché, said by every
holy tongue. So? Does that make it false?

She feels the bruises lift. She feels the cuts
lift. She feels the violence lift from her.
The rape, the exorcism, the gun she held
to her head, the knife she held to her wrist,
the burnt curls of poems—lift into
the sky like smoke. Her red blind rage
lifts, too (the violent shield). She's ready
to transform again, and when she does
she'll let the pain move through her into space
like the thunder of guns transmuted to a fugue.

Fox:

Metamorphosis: creatures growing
loud then silent. Where is Dante's Virgil?
Where's your psychopomp? Ovid, Blake,
or Plath? Let's say I'm Merwin in a fire
of dragonflies before the last tree dies.

Lily:

You're ruining my poem.

Robin:

And so our Lily follows Fox west
to Lake Michigan, and then into
the caves, which smell forgotten,
like a mausoleum built for fish.
What is "built"? All words seem strange, unhinged.
Her baby kicks, and damn! That foot is sharp.
An altar deep within the caves is lit
and trembles with the petals of anemones.

ACT III: LILY & THE FAUN

SCENE 1: CAVE RIDDLES, NO TIME

Crone Anemone:

Descend to caves unsuitable for
feathered beings. In darkness, the brown
chiropteran reign. Learn to see
with sound, to sense the columns overhead
and on the ground (like ancient cities drowned).
Your echolocation must be found
or else the hidden creatures will converge.
O limestone, riddles, pools of glass, resound!

Bats:

Like starlings in formation,
I perpetually change.
I shift with fortune,
power, and name.

With time I am scattered.
With time I am forged.
Yet I can't be shattered,
and I can't be stored.

Bat Lily:

My arms are star-bright,
my feet are bound.
I sing through heights
of broken sound.

My limbs are slaves,
my hands a salve.
My mind is made
of paper selves.

Bats:

I drip from above
to build from below.
While you observe,
I'll never grow.

The sea is my mother,
yet the earth is my sea.
I might grow taller
than a human being.

Bat Lily:

I'm replaceable, ethereal,
yet profess to be a god.
My instincts are too animal,
so I aspire to reason's law.

I'm hyperconscious, ironic,
won't let myself be saved.
Or my reason is cold, angelic,
yet I aspire to passion's wave.

What goes up must go down.
The pen is mightier than the sword.
Are you a man or a mouse?
Actions speak louder than words.

Make love not war.
Ashes to ashes, dust to dust.
At the end of the pecking order.
In god we trust.

Bats:

Blind as a bat.
Drowned as a rat.
Clean as a cat.
Right as a track.

Prickly as a briar.
Tricky as a mirror.
Deathless as a lyre.
The dark invented fear.

Darkness:

Antlers articulate America
As amoebic angst amplifies
Alluvial aquifer arterial allusions
Antigone alive Antigone American
Antihistamine antidepressant
Antimatter and antipathy antiseptic
Antisocial antiquity antiviral acrylic
Antichrist antidotes anticlimax
Antennae awoke AWOL[1] abulia atom
Anonymous automaton authority anonymous
American animism American alien anon
American avatar American ale
American authenticity American ailment

---

[1] Absent without leave, absinthe winter leaf, abomination wither lifeless, aimless willful laughter

American atrium
All-American allspice agoraphobia
American Airlines aerial
AIDS American ache
Astral American Adonis American
Aeneas American
Adam American Annabel-Lee American
Achilles American
Antihero American
AC/DC American amnesia
Ahhhmissyou American absolution
American Anarchy
Aquarian American a$$

Blinds big bad bard bitch
Begging blackbird beating blackhole
Blackmagic blacksheep blacklung
Blackwidow blacktop blankverse barbiturate
Blood blossoming below books big bad
Bummer bourgeois bumble bummer bastard
Blowfly beckoning bodies beckoning bombs beneath
Boredom beneath bondage bought
Beauty beneath being beautiful banshees
Being bark baptized being barbed being beehives
Battleaxe battleship battlefield Beyoncé butterflies
Bruise brutes birthday banners bling
Bitten betters bested bicycle bitch

Bible bitch bureaucratic bitch
Buzzard bitch blackhearted bitch
Bored bitch buzz buzz
Basic bitch bulimic bitch
Bipolar bitch blank bitch
Banal bitch blueberry bitch
Bar bitch bankrupt
Bitch Barbie bitch
Bitter bitch bacon
Bitch blow bitch bleed BFH[2]
Bat bitch bomb bitch bathos
Bitch bastard bitch
Bang bitch bang

Cannibals consume calicos consume cannibal calves
Caffeinated carbonated caesuras can't conceive
Contraband carbohydrate couplets can't
Cash cats candid camera cash crows can't
Cash cantos cash canticles can't create
Cash clouds cash clams cash creeds
Cash crooks cash creeks cash combines
Cash checks cash coronas COF[3]
Can't croon cradlesongs changeling charms
Can't croon commas cash commas create COF
Chiaroscuro chicken contrapuntal COF cue
Codices cue codes cue coils create code9
Create cages create caffeine cravings create

---

[2] Bitch from hell, balance feral hormones, broken female heroine, bleeding from head, bright fuckless hymen

[3] Crying on the floor, cryo-omniscient fräulein, cock on fire, cookies only fucks, cost of fucks, cranky ovary fucks, chaos OMG fucks, cold one fucks, completely ordinary fucks, come on fucks, creepy oldguy Ferrari, crone ontology foretelling, cave over forest

Coitus create creases cutting clotting
Cracking creaking cedars celebrating
Cypresses celebrating cynical cellulose cellphone
Cynical Cyclops cynical cyclones
Cynic cervixes cynic claustrophobia ceremonies
Cynic cerebellums cynic
Choruses conjuring chrysalises COF
Conjuring cocoons conjuring
Chromatic cunts cosmos cunts coconut
Cunts cocaine cunts catastrophic contraband
Cunt classroom cunt clairvoyant
Cunt creating classics creating canons
Cunt cult COF cunt come closer

Deer doll dominating darkness
Delirious dance dominating
Dilettante D&C[4] dirty drag dark-horse
Dumb druggy doppelgänger
Duh daisy duh delphinium
Duh diet diadem demented
Dementia democracy demise
Depress descend demon democracy
Desiccate destroy devil democracy
Devour death desire democracy
Dictation dictum d1ck democracy
Dynasty d1ck dagger d1ck dissociate
Deflower degrade dehumanize democracy

---

[4] Divide and conquer, Doritos and Cheetos, dragons and capriciousness

Decibel d1ck depression DTF[5]
Duende dick domestic dick
Dollar dick dat divine democrat
Dick dat delicate democracy dick
Drunk dandelion dick drunk damselfly
Dick drunk December dick
Drunk dildo drunk Dido DYWTGWM[6]
Demeter drunk double-dutch
Deja drunk delta dude dick
Don't deceive don't delete
Don't doormat don't door
Don't deodorize don't deify
Don't dear doll don't don't dream

Evergreen Eve ecstasy exhibitionist
Elemental eleven emblem ears
Everybody's elegant ears elegy ears
Elysium emotions ethos emojis
Elms embody ever ever emojis elephant
Emojis eggs ever Eros ever expanse emojis
Everglade ever erotic everybody emojis
Exotic estrogen ever-rage emojis
Every empty ever-conjuring everlasting emojis
Entrance entrance everything emoji emojis
Empire evanescent engine
Enters emoji elves enters emoji eels
Enters evening exodus emojis

---

[5] Down to fuck, drown to flunk, drank till falling, door trip funk
[6] Do you want to go with me? Do you will the god whips me? Do you wonder trees grow wispy memories?

Exhumes exultation emojis
Exhales emojis exhales emojis exhales eedyat
EZ era EZ earth EZ elk emojis
Ex-machina ex-ecosystem emojis
Extinction exhaustion expose EABOD[7]
Exorcism exile emojis embody
Exit evil emojis exit evangelist emojis
Exit essence exit epoch emojis
Epic etude emoji estrogen
Echo echolocation emoji
Every epithet every epitaph emoji
Every etched evolving ever
Ethereal eye

Fuck forever fuck fauns F&E[8]
Frozen funeral fifteen fetishes
Fem flickering feline fabulists
Fuck finding fem fertile fictions
F8 forms flying fornicating fierce
Fire-branded firestorm fire-eater fugue
Fire-monger firefly flight fluorescent FU
F8 foiled F8 frenetic F8
Flowered F8 forged fortuneteller
Fight flutter flux fight
F8 fight Furies fight flora
Fight fauna fight fish fight
Feathers fight foxes fight fire

---

[7] Eat a bag of dicks, earth a barge of dandelions
[8] Forever & ever, fornicate & eat, fritter & éclair, f8 & ecigs, fireball & email,
Frankenstein & emo

Fight forever fight flesh
Fight FU fight FI fight
Fusion fight fission fuck
Falcons fuck February fuck fighting
Fuck finite foreskin
Forms fusion fractal forest
Foxglove forming fossils
Flood freedom Facebook Farmville
Flood fillies flood foals flood families
Familiar foreign frosty
Felony forgery foamy
Fracking frazzled flannel fugly
Faustian fungus famine Funyuns

Gog gog gah geode grrl
Gave green gave grass
Gave gravitas gave gravity
Gave gangsta gave Greek
Gave grief gave Gabriel
Golden gyno gave georgics growl
Gave grades gave glorious genealogy gave guitars
Geometric gondoliers gave ginger gave geraniums
Gave Gaia garden glissando grade-A genome
Gave grammar gave grandeur gave ginormous
Glory glittering Gideon glaciers gave galaxies
Given God guns God given Genesis
Given genocide given guts given graves

Given guilt glass gore
Given ghouls given grails
Given gender given gay
Grenades given grape gum
Go go gadget getmethefuckouttahere given
Go go gadget god games gud games guy games
Goodbye games graffiti games garage games grace
Graceful graceless goddamn grace-it
Global games GOP games
Grow gutters grow garbage grow
Gr8 golden GDIAF[9] gosh goodness
Guru gurlz genius gr8 gr8 grrrrrrrrrrrr
GYPO[10] gentlemen!

Hear: Hurricane Hector Helen Hymen
Holy howl holy hood holy halogen
Holy haze holly halo hallucination
Heathen heather heaven heat
Human heat holy heat heretic hinterland
Holds hollow holds hoax holds hornets hypochondriac
Humming hypotenuse hallucination
Holds honor holds hyssop holds h8rs
Heroes hominid heroes herd heroes
Hell heroes h4xr heroes hair heroes
Hammer heroes heaven heroes hologram
Heroes Hulk heroes hurt hypothesis
Hegemony hypothesis hedonism hypothesis

---

[9] Go die in a fire, gourmet drink in a flask, gain dogma's intimate aesthetic fission
[10] Get your penises out, get your panties ogled, great yellow pansy omen

Hellebore hypothesis horn hysteria hype
Hour hype hand hype hair hype
Home hype ha ha
Haunt hawk ha ha
Harrow ha
Hang ha
Huh heavy heart ha ha
Have heavy heart ha
Hemoglobin high high hike
Have health have healing have
Horror have honey have hymns
Hiss honing hiss hardening
Herald home hertz HWU[11]

Ill illium Illiad illusion
Illustrious id ivory id
Ill id illustration iridescent
Irony iconic irony inner
Irony Icarus irony iron-born
Iron-age inborn imperfect
Iron icon iron incarnate ill ill
Iron inferno insomnia
Iron iamb IDK[12]
Inspired isosceles imperative
Imagination is invocation
Imagination is IDK
Imagination is interstitial

---

[11] Hey what's up, hello where's up, heave wilderness up
[12] I don't know, imagine daydream knight, illustrious delicious kinesiology

Imagination is interstellar
Imagination isn't illusion isn't infinite
Isn't inward isn't introspection
Is Inc. is isthmus IDK
Interconnected is increscent
Intensifying intensity interdependent
Inter-mutual instar IDK
Imagine imagination intellectual
Intimate instrument innamorata innamorato
Idol incubus indigo
Illuminated IDK itch
Involute into ice into images
Into infancy into isotopes into I

Jezebel jinx
Judas jinx
Jinni jinx joule
Jonquil jasmine jealousy
January jugular
Jupiter juju
Jesus jade jujitsu
Jugular justice
Jesus justice
JLT[13] jesting
Jesus jam
Jesus jar
Jesus jail

---

[13] Just like that, jester-like treason, junk lick trick

Jesus juncture
Jesus joy JLT
Jack-in-the-box joy
Jazz joy
Jargon joy JLT
Jig joy jejune joy
Juniper joy
Justice joy
Jewel June joy
Jay joy JLT juvenile
Jelly joy
Jackoff joy
Jesus Jesus Jesus jalapeño

King kilowatt king
Kangaroo king
Killdeer king kudzu
Kamikaze kiss K?
Kings kiss kerosene
Kiss kites kiss knights
Kiss knowledge kiss
Knots knotted knits
Knot knife knot kumquat
Knot kindred knot
Knock kind kook
Kaleidoscope key knuckle
Keen keep key kitty key

Karma kazoo K?
Kiss knows kick
Knows knowledge
Kungfu killable
KKK killable
Keening kids
Killable kleptos killable
KleptoCats killable
Kafkaesque KFC KMP[14]
Krunk Kabbalah
Kantian kind-hearted
Killable kitschy kyphotic
Katabolic knave

Ligatures labor liminal
Lessons lingual lion learning
Lip lineage lingers long
Lack luv lexicon laminated logos
Luv Lazarus luv labyrinth
Luv loam luv larynx luv language
Luminary language luminous language
Lunar lush lullaby lover LMFR[15] lush
Lover lucid leviathan lush libretto
Lush lazuli lush legacy lush lecture
Lush limelight lush lumn lung
Lore littered lithe livid lit laser
Litmus luck locket luck logarithm

---

[14] Kill me please, kindergarten mercury popsicle, kettle more popcorn
[15] Let's meet for real, lying man faux regal, liminal miracle fabulous REM

Luck locust luck loco luck
Lodestar luxurious linoleum
Lo lewd lepton liar legion l8
Legato leap lace lake l8r
Lady Gaga leap light lily leap lingo lily
Leap lingerie lily leap leaf
Lily lithe lily lilt lily licorice
Lily lunch lolz lily lymph lily
Lunacy lure lute lark leetspeak
L8 lily lucre liquor lover low
Lothario lounge lollipop
Loll linnet lizard line loll left
LBNR[16] life's licentious liberty

Magic mama microcosm muse
Majestic magenta metal muse
Minx minor miracle muse mountain
Music muse mysterious mycelium muse
Mythos Milky Way monolithic muse
Mood mitosis mint mood miniature mood
Molasses mood minion maze mood
Melody medium marvel mood medicine
Myriad myopic manifesto medicine mania
Marry March marry Methuselah
Marry manifesto marry mysticism
Marry marigolds marry mania malocclusion
Memory manga mmmm metabolism metempsychosis

---

[16] Laughing but not really, laughing beyond nothingness really, language beyond numbing reason, lunch by nefarious roadway

Metamorphosis m9 metaphor m9 metaphysics m9
Meditation m9 mercy m9 MLC[17] m9
Meta much mend much microwave much
Madonna much machete much Machiavelli much
Machismo much Maleficent much
Macabre machine maharajah MPD[18]
Magnolia makeup mourning muffin mnemonic
Mourning miracle mourning mutation
Morning myself morbid melancholy
Moth moon monolingual moon modem moon
Microchip moon milk moon meter moon matriarch
Moon menstruation moon madam moon mandrake
Malleable malingering macaroni monarch

Naked nameless nymphomaniac
Notorious neurotic novel neurotic
Necrotic nimbus nobody
Nonce nightingale negation nefarious
Negligee nectar needle need
Nation nasty nemesis nihilism
Neon nirvana non sequitor
Normative nonviolent noose
Nitrogen Nimrod nonchalance
Nominal nightmare next nightshade next
Nine nomad night nostalgic night
Nest night net night noun night
Numerology null November

---

[17] Midlife crisis, mental crucifix, merengue lemon confinement
[18] Multiple personality disorder, many people dreaming, maximum Peloponnesian drama

Noxious night nurse
Nondairy noncombatant nod
Nocturnal nod nettle nark narcolepsy
Nod nasturtium nod Nintendo
Narrow natal natural no1
Northwind northstar northcountry no1
Nothingness note nothingness nuclear
Nothingness neurotransmitters neurocognitive
No1 nothing nepotism never no no no NSA[19]
Nothingness nougat necklace
Nefertiti numinous
Narcissist numinous
Naaahmean? numbered nude

Obey orchestral orgasm
Oedipus orgasm obligatory orgasm
Ocean orgasm omnipotent orgasm
Orpheus orgasm oxygen orphan
Ornament overkill oyster
Origin outerspace origin outlier origin
Overseas origin overwrought ovum
Outrage ornate outrage online outrage
Obituary obscene occult octagon
Omega opera orchard
Original orgy OMGIH[20]
Original order OMGIH
Original opposite orifice

---

[19] No strings attached, numberless stars atrophied, numb sleepless aria
[20] Oh my god in heaven, oh my god in hell, odd myopic glow inside hornets, omega involution huntress

Orbital organic one one oblivion
One origin one opus one ozone
One other one obsolete
Off on off on October ovary
Old optician old oregano
Occupy ochre occupy ohm
Occupy olive occupy organ
Occupy Orion orthodox
Osmosis ossify o! owl ossify
O! Ox ossify o! oyster
Ossify o! obsessive o! orthorexia
O! orthopedic obsessive
Opioid obsessive o! ontology

Precious precocious prostitute psychic peeps
Pseudonym princess prances phasmophobic
Pariah penniless peony parody peeps pulse
Perfect peregrine periwinkle pyrrhic protest
Pyrrhic psycho pyrrhic pulchritude perfect persimmon
Permutation perfect preposition pretend pyromaniac
Priam pretend Plato pretend pomp plz pentameter
Pretend perfect play plumage plz psychedelic plz
Plural plethora polyphonic polymorphous
Polyunsaturated phat pregnant plz peridot
Pandora plz pantheon paradox parallax plz
Paris panties Paris pants-less pearly
Pathos passé peach patriarchy pupil

Plz p-nis peach pen peach penance p-nis
Plz Pan palindrome pencil paean plz
Pencil pagan pencil pretty petty pets pure
Pencil phallus pencil phantom pencil purr
Phantasmagoria pharaoh philodendron
Phoenix phonics photosynthesis pheromone pi
Piano pi pitch pi plague pi poem pi poison
Pi pollen pi pomegranate pi Poseidon pi
Porno porpoise postmortem postmodern potato
Possessed prig possessed prep possessed prince
Possessed porcupine positron power PTSD[21]
Power powder power prayer power prism power prophet
Power promise Prometheus plz pussy pussy pussy

Quaalude quantum quandary
Quantum quest
Quantum quarterly
Quantum quarterback
Quixotic quicksand quick-tempered
Quick-witted quip quorum
Quoth quotidian
Quoth quirky QLTM[22]
Quoth quietude quill
Quill quadratic quadruple QLTM
Quill quartet quill question
Quell quarto quatrain question
Queue quartz question

---

[21] Post-traumatic stress disorder, prowl Tarzan shirtless demigod, primal
treacherous spirits dancing
[22] Quietly laughing to myself, quasi linguist trembling malevolence

Queue quagmire question
Quaver qualified question
Quarantined quartz question
Quite quizzical
Question quite quirky
Quite Quixote
QFT[23] queeny
Quitter queeny quincunx
Quantum quintessence quince-cunts
Quotidian quintessence
Q quintessence
Queeny quintessence
Queeny quarrelsome quetzal

Rewrite rhapsody rewrite revelation
Rewrite renaissance rewrite revolution
Rewrite rhetoric rewrite ruthless
Rock rosary rock ritual rock righteous
Rock rhythm rock rhythm rock rock
Recoil redeem reform recreate refine
Repair repeat repent repel ruminate
Rotten reckoning Roman reckoning
Revolver reckoning ruby ruse rose restless
Romeo romance ruin rumor ruin reckoning restless
Ruin righteous ruin righteous ricochet restless
Righteous rambler running reciprocal raving restive
Raven rare rattle reforest regurgitate

---

[23] Quoted for truth, quell futile tirade

Rendezvous radiate reason radiate redwoods
Radiate repercussions repair repeat repent repel
Ruminate runes ruminate resilient resourceful
Riddle risk riddle river riddle ring riddle raccoon
Retrograde riddle rosin riddle root riddle rabies
Rise riddle rise risk rise rifle rise ribbon ROFLPIMP[24]
Rise rhizome rise rays rise reverse rise retrotextual
Rise retina rise respiration ROFLPIMP rise rest rise restroom
Rise requiem repugnant requiem REM requiem reject
Reincarnation r8p rise requiem regalia r8p
Requiem rainforest requiem r8p
Raspberry requiem rage requiem
R8pist rebirth

Sssssssssssssssssssssssssssssssssssssssssssssss
Sssssssssss satan sadist sawdust stardust saddest siren
Scream sin secret sin sepulcher sin suicide
Sarcophagus sin serial sin stigmata sin severe sin shame
Sermon shame sex shame sexy shameshrapnel shame
Simulacrum shame slither slip slap sloth
Slur smug smash sociopath switchblade sociopath
Seraphim superior supersonic superstar sociopath
Superstition surreal sepulcher smart sociopath
Smother smart solitary smart solo scar severe scar
Schizophrenic scorpion see skull see stimulant see stuttering
Sea-rose sea-anemone seascape seaweed season
Seed sentence seed syntax seed sequence seed

---

[24] Rolling on floor laughing pissing in my pants, realization of fabulous languid pointlessness in most principles

Sentimental seed septet seed said seed slay say
Seed say salient sonnet sonata sestina symphony
Say snake say serpent say smolder shoulder stream
Shimmer simmer shine soft shine sequin shine
Salvation saint SYOTB[25] salvation Saturn salvation
Sass salvation sapphire salvation sinew sing sang sung
Suckit sissy sister sissy siren sissy skylark SINGLE[26]
Swarm spinal swarm spirit swarm sperm swarm slaughter
Spell spider SWF[27] spell spindle spell SWF splendor spell SWF
Stamen spell storm spell stem spell stellar spell stillborn spell
Stigma spell stitch spell stag spell spring spell spark spanx
Spell Spartans spell specter spectral species spell salmon sand
Sanity shenanigan spell septuagenarian

Truth terrible truth tentacle truth taboo
Truth thankless truth thick totalitarian
Topless top-heavy topography tits
Transfigured tits truant tits
Tyro tits tautology trilogy trill
Treason trillions triumphant transfixed
Trident tsunami tyranny turbine
Tractor tramp tractor tempest tractor
Tintinnabulation trachea telekinesis
Tensile tenterhooks tequila thermodynamics
Thick throne thick thumbs thick thrum
Thrust time tight thunder tilt
Thor tizzy toga tirade turquoise tantrum

---

[25] See you on the battlefield, silt yearning oceanic thunder beaches
[26] Stay intoxicated nightly get laid everyday, sleazy in nightclubs gilded lazy ever-after
[27] Single white female, snow witch fantasy, sleep winging furiously

Tantric tarantula taboo talisman tabloid tattoo
Tantric tavern tale talon tale tangle tale tender
Tantric tarpaulin tender teeth tender toreador
Tongue telepathy therapy thaw TTYL[28]
Tetrameter thump tetrameter timbre
Tide twerk tide tourniquet tide translucent
Tide Troy's typhoon tympani Twitter
Troy's transgression transfixion transformation
Transubstantiation transpiration turtleneck
Tribute tune tune tune trance
Trace trajectory tranquil trajectory
Tumor trajectory thigh trajectory thorn
Third tampon taproot tamarack tanager

Utter ululate ultimate umbrage
Ultraviolet umbilical unyielding
Unchanging unadorned unconscious
Undefeated unending unbroken uncensored
Unorthodox unzips unattached
Uncanny unceremonious UFO
Uncertain unclothes unctuous
Underworld underage underworld
Underwear undying
Unfailing unforgettable utopia
Unraveling utopia
Unforgettable unfailing urinal utopia
Unto USA unto unlucky

---

[28] Talk to you later, triumphantly trashing your laundry

Urchins unto undulating
Unicorns unjust usage urban
Urethra upset uproarious
Unraveling underprivileged
Umber ugly
Unsympathetic ugly
Ungrateful ugly
Unbearable ugly unforgiven UFAB[1]
Unsafe undemocratic undesirable
Untried ugly ulterior ugly ulcer
Ulysses underbelly undertaker uncoiled
Understanding unfaithful unfortunate ugh
Unmanned ugh ultra ugh

Violent vainglory Valhalla violence
Variegated Vatican vaudeville violence
Vengeance voyage void violence
Volatile vodka vitreous vendetta
Virile victorious vendetta
Viking villain verve vendetta
Valor vicious valedictory Vulcan versus
Vigilante versus veteran
Versus voyeur versus
Venus vulnerable
Vestal violet vixen Venus
Vogue Venus voluptuous Venus
Vibrant vivace velvet Venus

---

[29] Ugly fat ass bitch, unappeased frat alpha bro, uncontrollable fluent ambitious boss

Veils vanity valentine
Veils Veda veils vascular
Vapor very vary vain vervain
Vaseline vain Valkyrie very
Violate violated victim very
Vessel vex vision virtual
Vision viol vision V4E[30]
Violin vision verb verity
Vision vernacular vision verdigris vine
Vibrato vine vagina vine vulva vine
Viburnum viceroy vineyard
Visitation vinyl vino
Vile viral video

Witch warring witch wintering
Witch wallowing witch
Wandering witch weaving witch
Weeding witch whispering witch wild-eyed
Witch-hazel wizened women
Witness woman wistful wanting
Woman wry woman withered
Woman worldly woman
Woven wrought winnowing
Wizard woman womanly woman
Wondrous wailing wondrous
Wallflower wondrous whatever
Weak weird weary waning whore

---

[30] Virgins 4 ever, vegetables 4 eating

Wasteland whore wicked WTF[31]
Wild whitewashed wild whiskey
Wildfire wildflower wildlife wile we will
West Wind wisteria willow we will
Wolf wolverine will-o'-the-wisp we will
Winchester workhorse workaholic we will
Write writhe worship we will w8
Waterfall watercolor waterlily
Welcome why when who what where
Weep well-made well-spoken wellspring
Whip-it wisdom whelm wisdom
Wheeling whimsical wisdom
Whirligig whirlpool whippoorwill

Xylem xtreme X
Xanthic xtreme XX
Xenolith xtreme XXX
Xanthippe xing
Xylomancy xroads
Xylogenous xroads
Xyloglyphy xroads
Xylography xtc
Xtra x-chromosome
X-ray xtra
X-mas xtra
XO XYZ[32]
XXX

---

[31] What the fuck, why treacherous frenemies, want true freedom
[32] Xamine your zipper, x-rated young zealots

Xenodochial
Xenagogue
XYZPDQ[33]
Xiphopagus
Xenial
Xanax
XGF[34] Xerox xs
Xyster xs
Xenogamy xs
Xeric
Xanthocomic
Xyloid
XL

You yellow you
You yuppie
You yearling you
Yokel yammering yesman
You yo-yo
Yew yucca
Yummy yolk
Yielding yolk
Yearning yelp
Yesterdays Yahoo
Yesterdays yonder
Yesterdays yield
Yesterdays youth

---

[33] Xamine your zipper pretty darn quick, xo you zzz plz dancing queen
[34] X girl friend, xylophones getting frantic

Yes yogurt y'all
Yes yoga y'all
Yes yelling y'all
Yes yowling
Yes yes yes
Yesses yawn
Ye Yahweh
Ye Yanni
Ye Yvonne
YAPA[35]
YOLT[36]
YWAPOM[37]
Yeah you

Zeether zither zillion
Zirconium zizzle Zeus
Zigzag zodiac
Zipper zodiac
Zipper zeppelin
Zipper zephyr
Zing
Zero
Zing
Zen
Zing
Zygote zounds
Zombie zounds

---

[35] Yet another pointless acronym
[36] You only live twice
[37] You want a piece of me

Zoroastrian zounds
Zonked
Zucchini zonked
Zealot zonked
Zilch zilly
Zonked zest
Zinc zing
Zion
Zany
Zex ZOT[38]
Zap zap ZOT
ZOT zappppp

Lily:

Zzz

---

[38] Zero tolerance, zoo testicles, zeitgeist of tintinnabulation

SCENE 2: OVID, MICHIGAN, 1994

Lost in the forest, Lily gives birth to a faun.

Lily:

In a leafy swoon   among the stag-shaped
    lichen   I rest my head
against pine bark   beyond marshes   beyond
    creeks   where ghosts of graylings jump
        where the dead uncross at dawn among the vines   and a faun
human above   animal below   is led
by gravity into blue

                                    while walking alone
            in the forest   my water breaks   bursts beckons   Faun
feels the primordial   water-universe
seize   contract   drain
                            where there was darkness

there was weightlessness   but now the surge

of matter   flesh forcing   the earth's nest
        pulses green   pulses high C
                    sharp
                        pulses I am breath

Faun:

The cattle's bones turn into wrens. Then
I'm a shadow's shadow. Animal is human and human
animal: animal-born, animal-raised, animal-taught.

Wrens embody animal thought with human rage.
Wrens speak in the language of power against
the language of power. Now wrens

laugh at the destruction of the world and dress me
in prisms. Now death is a sea of animal-light
above the flying bones of cattle.

Archer and Optician hear Lily's screams and run into the forest. Optician sees the faun first.

Optician:

Manbuck   deerfootedhumanface

    horsehuman   hornsapien

trick this   trick   trick dreaming   I

'm   dreamaging wakeup   wakthfkup

dudefaun

    old panor   some   satiremyth

ologybro   buckman   songoat   wake

clovenhoof   ohno clovenhoof   ohjeez

us horns and a   clovenhoof   oh devil

                                  DEVIL
                           DEVIL
                DEVIL
DEVIL D
         EVIL   EVIL

               EVIL

The faun bolts. They follow the trail of blood to Lily.

Lily:

It's time for my body   to surrender   born
red animal   knot   human   not   alien
I know   I'm like a wren   in stillness   worm
hammered   leaf breathing   a salmon   sea breathing   saline
my hands are

        open   my eyes are

        riddles   stranger

hands reaching up   & up   my harvest swells   alone
the first woman's   bloody hands reach   five   eight   ten
fingers dripping
         why am I ashamed?
                           without
blood   I'm barren   without blood I'm a machine
      but not today   today I leave the earth   & enter

a red world of beasts with clouds floating under

Root Song:

Red, red, red hollow
Home. Flight through
Mycelium bone, flew
Through the galaxy foam,

Soared into a red sphere,
A red-veined ocean dome,
A home, a home, a home.
A mother's primordial fear

Of half-things, unformed, too formed,
Winged, hooved, horned & the stone
In their hearts when a faun is born
And walks without a cry. There's a storm

Brewing in their heads. O grist,
O mother, O –vid, O –bey, "Oh!"
They said, that's all they said, "Oh!"
A satyr, a god is born to this.

Crone Anemone, sun-bloated, swoops, blinding Optician and Archer as they carry Lily to the truck.

Crone Anemone:

Between worlds, burst light from fallen leaves & watch
a chorus of starlings travel through
tree roots (red to yellow, green to blue).
Burn hydrogen, helium, gone. Faun,
unfurl like a butterfly pumping
skeletal wings from a chrysalis. Weave
halos, gold vines melting to pink trout stretching
to white petals. Thread!
Plants, animals, skies, fish, insects, girl, faun.

Optician:

I see a woman, graceful through the trees,
    graceful with long hair blue in the sun.
        She climbs with long acrobatic limbs.
The eyes of branch scars and river stones divinely voluminously
spark the eternal woman's form, revealing her eight eyes—
Skull, wings, shoulders, head, and navel—

    Because a devil is born, while Lily dies.

    I search the underbrush.
    I graze a horn with my fingertip.

    Because a devil is born, and my daughter dies.

It's impossible to sense where our bodies end
because we're becoming large, and we're becoming
no longer us, but all.

Crone Anemone:

Dress her in anemones, earthen round saplings!
Plant her under! A hundred years gone
to her calves. Two hundred years & great pines spring
while passenger pigeons roar. A thousand years
buried to the neck.

Archer:

What creature stalks what creature claws
    blood over blood her cold body creat
        ure of Death in the branches I hear h
er cold body blood over blood the branches
stolen stealing a soul stalks the starlings c
    law Death in the branches stalks what
in the what bran chwhat stalk swhat
        blood her cold body lacks oh hospit
           oh hospital emerge over the branches
        bloodove rblood sirens emergency

        This is an emergency

        This is an emergency

        This is an emergenc

Crone Anemone:

Wound-eyes, phantom limbs
Twitch once, twice. Hum other worlds
through maples. Hum the distant chainsaw air &
watch Wood Anemones
like snow, erase the sky. Stand, Archer, your sixth
    finger leading you to where I hide.

        Red, streak Archer's beard,
severed roots.
                    Archer's Fear,
        birth a cloud of dragonflies.

Dragonflies:

The yellow flower is the death flower.
The scarlet flower is the open flower.

The magnetic field is my dream field.
The cornfield is my lost field.

I'm all grass. She's linnet wings
I'm pure delta. She sings:

    Into hedges
      Into sedges
         Into stone
        Into foam
            Bring me
        Bring me
      O bring me

        Starlings!

Faun disappears into the woodihlkhks into the woodts the woodZ. Archer gathers up Lily's body. She's butterflthlies a rasp of paper bags. Starlings follow.

Starlings:

She fails to poetry   Qua absolute zero
Fails to poetry   Bright animal
Moments   Of breath

Thinking death is   Above not rooted
Distance isn't   Far or near it's
A nether   Airplane

Azure qua sky or   A serpent's heart
Death symbol   Poem qua ruin
Corpse   Qua qua

Would you like a paperhuman with your paperwork? Would you like a paper paper with your paper? Would you like to see your human bleed in a truck speeding toward Sparrow hospital? Would you like to see a sparrow on a wire speaking human?

Sparrow:

Human.

Would you like forty-five minutes of "I'm dreaming-ing"? Of "clovenhoof-ing"? Of a dying woman's silentcastle? Of bloodsparrows on the seat of a Ford diesel truckkk? How about some climactic charcases? Poelice shoutravens?

> *Archer runs a red lighthammer, breakbolts, highbeams, godspeeds*

> *Lily until she's a*
> > *whiteblanket wireprincess,*

until the drumbeeps multiply and cease, multiply and ease, until the beepsparrows

> *cease into polite lil' wingmachines.*

Meanwhile, the faun follows Crone Anemone, star-like, to the farmhouse.

Crone Anemone:

Break and drink. Drink and break and dance
the rooms. Crash
Precious Moments Figurines, Home Interior Angels,
Porcelain Cats. Piss rivers and watch wood grains
crack, green, and rootlings grow. Sprout anemones from beds, rugs,
while floorboards pop with frogs.

Faun:

The Immense Filigreed Spirits (IFS) are the pyromaniacs
of our burnt martyrs, whose magnified movie posters

recognize nothing. They demolish the value of literature
and the authority of eloquent syntax. Their power

is modal and performative with a bourgeois
hatred for revolution. They turned Mallarmé

into a banker. They are born of two disapproving
evangelists before whom your arguments are evil

undulations. Ahhh! Their greatest power lies in unemployed
factory workers and a fear of liberals. The Immense

Filigreed Spirits consume nasty women who hail from the University
of Feverish Insomnia with vaginas full of protest signs.

Their ideal prodigality is a masterpiece of cataloguing, for the IFS
lie looking for the space of yesterday, the speed speed speed

of muscle cars. The IFS are the ones in jubilation
of fried Oreos melted into a social class, yourself,

a carnival willing itself peculiar and impoverishing everyone. The IFS
are Lords of the Curatorial, who reanimate revolutions

of the indefinable, who make their own excremental magic.
The IFS are cherries gleaming with flies, an attack on poetry's

instant electric insurrection. They are against the yes
where life and death swing, against the sixth dimension

of breathing bodies seeking words, page, line, and gesture—

Faun dresses in a loose business suit, pulls some boots over his furry legs and walks toward the tiny town of Ovid. There is only Main Street Pizza, the Ovid Bar, an IGA, and a gas station.

Faun:

The imagination of night is incalculable.
The Immense Filigreed Spirits (IFS) radiate your eyes

and love/hate your cruelty, for your mothers
are their eager delicious secretaries and your fathers

are their squandered delirious proletariat, and on your graves
live infamous words: Born. For those in the IFS's

imagination employ death. Their machines are fueled
by the blood of your children; for also the imagination now

serves the IFS, and oceans, clouds, and snowflakes serve the IFS.
The IFS are the searchlight of the self. Anyone who interrupts them

will disappear into their dark bellies against the walls
of flooded cities while the IFS rest

upon the clouds in heavenly bivouacs. For billions frame
their wisdom and offer them gift baskets for Administrative

Professionals Day; for they have been awarded the rumbling
of airplanes and semis in moribund concrete palaces

by 3-D gaming systems, fathers of the Atari and Nintendo;

For the IFS have suddenly hinged a splendor-sword of battling machines

with a breast for a steering wheel, ourselves swept like wild beasts;
for the demise of unhappiness has been sold to us

half price with a free bag of victory butterflies riding horses of air.
The IFS will barricade matter in relation to a *logopoeia* hailed

soluble itself. The IFS will spit out your bones and feed them
to your children, and the IFS will not be dethroned; their privileges

will not be lost because they have eaten your eyesight
and stolen your social security number. Golden is the world of the IFS,

impunity is their limit, and "The Good Farmer Availeth Vanity"
is their mantra, which is a corruption of originality

and poetry's absence forever within. For your desires
are in the IFS's imagination and your disappointments

feed the IFS, as the words they masticate are your meals,
polyunsaturated, made of your ancestors' tongues; for your imaginations

belong to the IFS and only your fear belongs to you, for the IFS is neither
yours, nor burning, but inside you shivering and tearful.

At last Faun arrives in Ovid, watching as people crash their pickups at the site of his horns. Hunters grab their rifles; women grab their children. Still, Faun speaks:

Faun:

> The twilit sky defines hatred as a happy conundrum, fuzzy
> and nebulous, like diamonds mixed with concrete. Do you hear
>
> Baby Jesus's serenity? You only hear the IFS's automated
> voice recognition system: "To speak with a representative,
>
> say, 'Eternity.' I'm sorry. I can't hear you." This is a war cry
> to reform legislation and to theoretically revalue the feminine element
>
> which is now defined as negation. You must dig for against-ness and
> manifestos of enmity and forget oblivion and irony is simply too petty—

A few men cock their rifles, shouting "Devil, devil!"

Faun:

What of delicious manna handcrafted as mime thyme moralism?
What of gluttonous smoking railways and nocturnal capitals?

Shoot your guns, small fish. You are too weak to be tossed by the pleasure
of revolution. The Immense Filigreed Spirits propel the wind

like an enthusiastic crowd, tumbling, incendiary. The future delivers
antiquarians, secondhand brokers and innumerable museums jostling

with great ferocity once a year. The IFS admit every *(bang!)* poison,
crucified dreams and broken catalogues of young men and their *(bang!)*.

The IFS's nobility is you daily passing by libraries with the best
of you gutted and *(bang! bang!)*.

For your future wounds are wonderful to the IFS who want nothing
but your patriotism as valiant and useless as a flood of *(bang!)*.

The thunder of shots continues, leaving Faun bleeding, feeling the light lengthen into finger-spindles. Leaving an aura of red on the asphalt, Faun, like all demigods, is unspeakably beautiful in death. Unblemished skin and sharp features contrast with full lips, and horns glitter in the sun. Like Dionysus with long curling hair, Faun is lush and androgynous. So the townspeople take off the business suit. They touch the thin and slightly muscled arms, and then they take off the undershirt. Ribs show through the skin of a child. Fur begins at the hips where the skin grows thicker. They pet soft legs, tap on hard and delicate hooves, which smell like woods after heavy rain. The townspeople are in love, ashamed and crying. They don't know what to do. Most of them get in their cars and drive away, trying to forget what they saw. A few of the hunters stay behind. One of them gathers up the body and digs a grave. It rains for two straight months. The crops are lakes; the streets are rivers; the inhabitants are gone.

While it rains and rains, Optician changes Lily's bandages and checks her mouth for unswallowed pills.

Flood:

>   milk   vs.   cash
>   yolks   in   hand
>   cold   land
>   crows caw   ice   opus
>   halo   of   rain
>   irises   undo   omens
>   lure   six   pain-filled
>   domes   hearing
>   rah   agog   grrr   yawp
>   eek   into an   odd   larynx
>   not   rivers   dead   lungs
>   sing
>   of   pink
>   f or   love   only
>   acid   foreign
>   scars
> sand   talking
>   lucky   ilium
>   inky   caves
>   mane of   flames
>   eggs of   idolatry
>   faun of   salt of
>   iron   home of
>   sure
>   hawks

Crone Anemone:

Absorb dead tree memories, brown grass, larvae
drown on milkweed. Rats, drown. Computers,
float through the forest.

Flood:

calx drowns
　aeons drown
　　ranunculus drowns
　　　fools drown
　　　　ions drown
　　　　　stars drown
　　　　　　harp crown

Crone Anemone:

Float Faun's bones through the flooded corn field and
rain hard. Float vases full of dead flowers, sympathy cards, ashes, and
rain hard. Float pine's waterlogged roots, rooftops,
into the great sea of Lake Michigan where things sink
and unspool and are nibbled by Asian carp.

Forge new shores.

Flood:

m ercy
e ther
r ain   e
c logs   v
y our   perfect e ternal

f ace   love   r
I 'm   eas y
s ly   a   t
h ope   s h orelines
e i ther/or
n
g

s ummer birds
t
o
p

162

Lily, Archer, and Optician are living at her aunt's house until the flood recedes.

Lily:

I gave birth to a god   & they killed him

said he never was

sprayed Roundup on flowers
        blooming from hardwood floors   hacked elms
springing from dressers
everything disappears
like how my aunt photoshops her face   until it's a veil
 of soul-making   ageless   showing only her mad
blue eyes   we perceive what we believe   it's sad

But I know things now   collective things   mammal nest
    things   bee hive snail shell things
I won't give up
my wrist-scratch ribbons pink   I put pressure on
the wound   the starlings peck peck peck

        no I won't apocalypse
        I won't   vanish
I'll get up each day &   I'll get up   & step
        step   livingly
& lay to rest my god
my supernal   my home

Lily slides her aunt's rowboat into the river and paddles toward Ovid. By nightfall, the river swells through flooded forests. Crone Anemone floats inside Faun's skull, which is hooked on a low hanging branch.

Crone Anemone: *(with wet brown petals)*

Seek   it shines

       nymph   mass of s

          truimph   horns fa

     Swoon   flute

          tangled   seeking the la

Faun's Skull:

Crone Anemone:

Eclogue

bye   dream

nymph   die   adam

Become   bitch   until

fire

Return

Lily picks up Faun's skull and puts it on.

ACKNOWLEDGMENTS

I would like to thank the following journals, in which scenes of this play first appeared: *Columbia Journal*; *Fence*; *Forklift, Ohio*; *Gulf Coast*; *Hiram Poetry Review*; *Newfound*; *The Ocean State Review*; *Orion*; and *South Florida Poetry Journal*.

Additionally, this book would not exist without my spouse, Michael Barach, who helped me to revise it a thousand times. I also appreciate the insightful comments of my poetry group from Tallahassee: Carrie Lorig, Sandra Simonds, and Nick Sturm. I also owe a special thanks to Barbara Hamby, who found the heart of the book and pushed me to make it better, and Jennifer Schomburg Kanke, who gave me the confidence to pursue my vision. I also wouldn't have been able to discover the form of this book without Joyelle McSweeney's vibrant and original plays in verse. This manuscript also benefitted considerably from the following summer residencies: The Hambidge Center for Creative Arts and Sciences, The Hill House Artist Residency Program, and the Time and Place Award in France.

This book also relies heavily on artists from the past, including phrases from William Blake, Martin Buber, Albert Camus, Claude Debussy, John Donne, Ralph Waldo Emerson, Robert Frost, Stéphane Mallarmé, Henri Matisse, Ovid, William Shakespeare, Percy Bysshe Shelley, Sir Philip Sidney, Henry David Thoreau, Walt Whitman, William Carlos Williams, and W.B. Yeats. And thank you to Ovid, Michigan for haunting me, both dreaming and awake.

BRANDI GEORGE grew up in Ovid, Michigan. Her first book of poetry, *Gog* (Black Lawrence Press, 2015), won the gold medal in the Florida Book Awards, and her poems have appeared in such journals as *Gulf Coast*, *Prairie Schooner*, *Best New Poets 2010*, *Ninth Letter*, *Columbia Poetry Review*, and *The Iowa Review*. She has been awarded residencies at Hambidge Center for the Arts and the Hill House ISLAND residency, and the Time & Place Award in France. She teaches writing at FSW in Fort Myers, Florida.